CARRIER PILOT

USS Hornet CV-12 1944

BILLY BUSH

iUniverse, Inc.

New York   Bloomington

Carrier Pilot
USS Hornet CV-12 1944

iUniverse books may be ordered through booksellers or by contacting:

iUniverse
1663 Liberty Drive
Bloomington, IN 47403
www.iuniverse.com
1-800-Authors (1-800-288-4677)

ISBN: 978-1-4502-5566-0 (sc)
ISBN: 978-1-4502-5568-4 (ebook)
ISBN: 978-1-4502-5567-7 (dj)

Printed in the United States of America

iUniverse rev. date: 9/15/2010

TABLE OF CONTENT

Acknowledgement

Many friends have generously contributed to this effort. My wife is to be commended for her patience and assistance. In particular, I would like to thank Bob Lass, a friend of many years. Without his encouragement, support, and assistance, this narration might never have been completed. Kent Winchester was most helpful with comments and support. And, a special thanks to Ted Spitzmiller for his interest, encouragement, motivation and generous assistance.

*** All photos are US Navy unless noted otherwise ***

Foreword

Without contemporaneous written accounts, we might know nothing of the courageous stand of Leonidas and his Spartans in the Pass at Thermopylae. Xenophon inscribed for history the retreat of The Ten Thousand from Persia. We can read David Chandler's magisterial Twentieth Century history of Napoleon's campaigns, but if we want to know what the winter retreat from Moscow in 1812 was really like, we read Sergeant Adrien Bourgogne's account of the Grande Armée crossing the ice at Berezina. The futile courage of the charging Light Brigade at Balaclava was recorded on the spot by William Howard Russell. Peter Thompson's private memoirs uniquely describe the battle at the Little Bighorn. Much of what we know about World War I in the desert, we learned from Lawrence of Arabia's contemporary journal.

The book you are about to read comes from that long tradition of combatants describing their wars. This time the warrior is Commander Billy Bush of the United States Navy. Here is an eyewitness account by a naval aviator in the Pacific during World War II, telling the story of one individual's contribution to winning the war.

World War II was the cataclysmic event of the Twentieth Century. Everything else pales in comparison. No one will ever know precisely how many people died as a result, but surely more than sixty million. Subsequent history from that day to this is driven by the upheaval it caused. The world emerged a different place, one deeply scarred and less innocent.

As World War II fades from living memory into history and myth, other names for it may arise. Perhaps it will be called, as the Russians have always called it, "The Great Patriotic War." Or maybe it will be known as the "Second Thirty Years War," for future historians may well see the years from 1914 through

1945 as one continuous war, broken only by a temporary lull between 1918 and 1939. Or perhaps it will be known as the "Twentieth Century War".

What we can predict with confidence is that the first person accounts of the men and women who fought it will become more important as time passes. This book, and the diaries from which it comes, is one such record and we are fortunate that Billy Bush decided to share it with us and with the historians who will follow.

My personal experience has been that World War II combat veterans seldom spoke about their experiences until fifty years or more after the war, so awful was the time. The memories of those veterans faded and clouded during the intervening half century and lacked immediacy. Bush's book does not suffer that malady. Although possessed of a remarkable memory, the stories you are about to read are based on his diaries, faithfully kept during his time in the Navy. Everything you will read here is drawn from that contemporary record, seasoned perhaps by the wisdom that comes with passing years, but still immediate, accurate, and vivid because it comes from those diaries.

Don't expect to read here self-aggrandizing stories about Bush. Not that kind of man, he tells anyone who asks that he, "was just doing my job." That is true, as far as it goes. He *was* just doing his job. His job, though, was dangerous, required exemplary courage, and demanded highly honed professional skills. Commander Bush's job was not for the faint of heart. Lifting bomb-laden airplanes off the short decks of aircraft carriers, flying to targets by dead-reckoning, dive-bombing targets that shot back; then returning—again by dead reckoning, sometimes after dark—to a tiny heaving deck in the middle of the Pacific Ocean is not a job many could do. His contributions required much more than he admits in these pages.

Nor will you find here, unless you read carefully and between the lines, anything about the emotional trauma he endured. War is an ugly business and no one escapes its maw untarnished and undamaged. People on all sides die sudden, violent deaths or suffer horrible injuries and the ones who live to bear witness never escape the pain.

Reading this book, you enter the world of a young American on his way to war. Looking out through his eyes, you experience his trajectory from enlisting in the Navy to his cockpit that June evening in 1944 when the Americans found the Japanese fleet in the Philippine Sea. If the Battle of Midway was the turning point in the Pacific War, the Battle of the Philippine Sea was the point of no return for the Japanese Empire. After that engagement, the outcome of the war at sea was sealed; it was only a matter of time. Commander Billy Bush received the Navy Cross (the nation's second highest honor) for his bravery that evening, but before he could write about it in his diary, he had to fly back to his aircraft carrier. It was dark, he faced 350 miles of open ocean and he was low on fuel.

I'll stand clear now, and let him tell you about it.

Kent Winchester

This book is dedicated to the young, patriotic members of Bombing Squadron Two who did not return.

Introduction

World War Two was a period of unprecedented turmoil throughout the world. Most nations had chosen sides in a struggle which clearly defined good and evil. Obviously, the United States and its Allies were on the side of good, and the enemy was on the side of evil.

This narrative describes some of my experiences as a young man, with a strong feeling of patriotism, and love of country during that war. It covers a period starting prior to the Japanese attack on Pearl Harbor on 7 December 1941, to the capitulation of the Axis Powers in 1945. I wanted to make an important contribution to the war effort. I wanted to make that contribution as an aviator.

During my combat experience, I was presented with opportunities that few individuals would have. My contributions toward the defeat of the enemy were at a level substantially above that of the average member of the military. Although those experiences have long since become ancient history, I have believed they might be of interest to subsequent generations.

In reality, this project was really for my own satisfaction. I discovered that as I neared the end of this document. In the past, it had been difficult to discuss the personal experiences that my Squadron Mates and I had. The writing of this book has substantially reduced the reluctance to think and talk about those experiences.

Billy Bush   June 1, 2010

Reflections

It was June 20, 1944, 1900 hours (7:00 PM), in a tropical sky, 450 nautical miles northwest of Guam. We were at 16,000 feet. In the cockpit, the sun was still shining brilliantly. On the surface, daylight was turning to dusk, and the large Japanese carrier, Zuikaku, was maneuvering frantically at flank speed in anticipation of the forthcoming attack. We would have preferred to be at 18,000 feet or higher to reduce further the danger of the intense antiaircraft fire we were encountering, but we were at the absolute maximum limit of our aircraft's range. If we were to return to our ship, USS Hornet CV-12, after the attack, it was necessary to conserve fuel by approaching and attacking our target from the lesser altitude. In a moment, we would be rolling into our dives, and attacking the most important target we would ever encounter.

Every Navy dive bomber pilot dreamed of this moment. It was the moment I had visualized, and anticipated since I was sworn in as an Aviation Cadet on that March day in 1942.

There were many memories and events between earlier childhood thoughts and the events that were about to take place. This journey actually started many years before, as a child, when my mother appeared on the scene in the summer of 1927 with her third husband, Romey Taylor, an individual who would have a major influence in my life. My brother Jack and I had been living with our grandparents in Pueblo, Colorado during the formative years of our lives. The following years would be a dramatic change from the stability we had known.

Romey was a hard working 22 year old, only 15 years older than I, who got a temporary job as a truck driver that summer in Pueblo delivering sand and gravel for a Pueblo construction company. His pay was only $3.00 per day. In September, he was offered a job in Sandpoint, Idaho as a steam shovel operator on a highway construction project. When his new employer sent him $100.00, in advanced wages, via Western Union, we departed almost immediately for the northwest. That $100.00 was, of course, worth many times what it was in today's dollars.

On a pleasant September day, in a tan, open air Paige automobile, with an oil cloth type top, our belongings strapped to the front fenders and running boards and a newly adopted three legged dog, we departed for northern Idaho. It was a journey never to be forgotten by a seven year old boy. Our trip, more than 1000 miles, took us north through Denver, Cheyenne, Wyoming, and west. Many of the roads were unpaved. In southern Idaho, we paralleled the Snake River, and eventually traveled through the rolling wheat fields of eastern Washington and into northern Idaho. There were several months in Sandpoint, the winter in Wallace, and then Coeur d'Alene in the spring of 1928.

We were nomads. In seven years, we lived in three different towns and in ten different houses. We always rented furnished dwellings. They could hardly be called homes. All we owned could be carried in a few suitcases. They could be moved in one load in our car. Although Romey was a dedicated worker, steady jobs were hard to find. He had four different jobs in the first year we were in Idaho. The fourth job was that of a bus driver, one which he would hold for most of his working career.

Romey usually worked seven days a week with an occasional day off. On those days, he associated with acquaintances who were involved with aviation in Spokane, Washington and at the small airport in Coeur d'Alene. I was allowed to accompany him on numerous occasions, and at an early age, I was filled with the excitement of flying airplanes.

My first airplane ride was in the summer of 1931. Some barnstorming pilots with two undefined biplanes came to Coeur d'Alene, offering flights from an alfalfa field on the north side of town alongside Government Way, for the modest price of one dollar. That dollar, of course, represented by many times the value of the current dollar.

Romey was generous in supporting the venture. My brother and I sat side by side in the front cockpit. The ride consisted of taking off, making a wide sweeping turn over the town and the western edge of Lake Coeur d'Alene, and returning to the alfalfa field. It was only a ten minute ride, but it was exciting, an adventure that I remember clearly almost 80 years later. There were other occasional plane rides, each one memorable.

However, it was not until the fall of 1939 that several events took place which would have a major influence on my life. That summer, I had been working for the U.S. Forest Service on a white pine blister rust control project, deep within the Coeur d'Alene National Forest, on Nicholas Creek. At the end of the season, I returned to Coeur d'Alene and enrolled in the local Junior College. I also enlisted in the local National Guard unit to earn a little extra money, and get additional college credit.

September 1, 1939—German troops invade Poland, starting World War Two. I remember the event well, but the thought of it influencing my life was remote.

I have been a fortunate individual throughout my life, and one of the most fortunate events occurred in December 1939. Margery Ann Hutsell, another student at the Junior College, and an acquaintance I had known in Spanish classes in high school, accepted my invitation, on very short notice, to attend a formal dance, sponsored by the local DeMolay chapter of the Masonic Lodge. She accepted. The date was December 26, 1939.

Marge did not have a formal dress, but she borrowed one from her Aunt June. It was a cerise colored taffeta dress. The sweet pea corsage I presented for the occasion matched perfectly. I was 19 years old and Marge was about to turn 18. It was the beginning of a more than seventy year romance.

In the summer of 1940, Marge enrolled in the Civilian Pilot Training (CPT) course offered by the Junior College, the only woman in the class of ten. They received training, flying J-3 Piper Cubs on floats, on Lake Coeur d'Alene. It offered a vast area for takeoff and landing, and they learned to sail instead of taxiing. She received her private license after completing the course. I worked for the U.S. Forest service again that summer. I had yet to consider becoming an aviator.

The summer of 1940, for me, was another blister rust control project. It was in the St. Joe National Forest, about 100 miles from Coeur d'Alene, on Poor Man's creek.

Although, it had been my intent to return to school for another year, my plans were changed, and as a member of the local National Guard unit, I was looking forward to a year in the military at Ft. Lewis, Washington along with all of my buddies. But, that near "catastrophe" did not occur. In reality, it was one of the most favorable events in my life.

I quit my job with the Forest Service in late September, and reported for active duty along with all of the other members of my National Guard unit. I failed the physical examination because of a right inguinal hernia.

My friends all went off to Ft. Lewis, Washington for a year, and I went back to school. My National Guard unit continued its training during the next twelve months. Instead of being released from active duty after a year, my friends found themselves being retained for an indefinite period. In late November 1941, they were aboard ship bound for the Philippines, and were one week west of Honolulu when the Japanese bombed Pearl Harbor. Their group was immediately diverted to Australia for temporary duty. They eventually fought in a very dirty war, participating in battles in New Britain, New Guinea and the Philippines. I would subsequently fight the same war, with equal or greater casualties, but aboard a U.S. Navy ship.

In October, 1940, the president of the Junior College learned of my physical problem and took it upon himself to contact a local surgeon on my behalf. The surgeon was also the owner of one of the small hospitals in Coeur d'Alene.

After a consultation with the doctor and a discussion about my financial assets, he volunteered to correct the hernia and provide all of the necessary medical care for one hundred dollars. That was one half the amount I had saved from my summer's employment with the Forest Service. Wages in 1940 were modest—fifty cents an hour, with ninety cents per day deducted for room and board. Board and room involved living in tents and eating in a cook shack that was little more than a tent. I had done well to save two hundred dollars.

In October 1940, my hernia was repaired in facilities and by techniques which by today's standards would be considered rather primitive. Dr. Sturgis performed the task; and to this day, there have been no undesirable effects. The only indication of the incident is a jagged six inch scar with smaller circular scars alongside. The circular scars were caused by large stainless steel clips which had been used instead of conventional stitches to close the incision.

I was back in school for the fall and winter of 1940-1941. The curriculum included a course in Civilian Pilot Training (CPT). In reality, it was a program to provide a reservoir of potential military pilots for some time in the future.

I enrolled in the course and was able to spend forty delightful hours flying J-3 Piper Cubs from the small dirt airport in Coeur d'Alene. That was followed by Advanced CPT at Felt's Field in Spokane, Washington during the summer of 1941 where we flew Waco UPF-7s. They were open cockpit biplanes with 200 H.P. radial engines. The syllabus was directed primarily toward aerobatics.

Figure 1. The Piper J-3 Cub was flown by the author in the Civilian Pilot Training (CPT) Program 1941.

Flying the Waco really made us feel as though we were "aviators"!! The open cockpits, leather helmets, and goggles, the wind in one's face, and the thrill of performing slow rolls, snap rolls, loops, chandelles—a glorified wing over. EXCITEMENT! My instructor, "Bunny" Dunn enjoyed pulling the throttle back on occasion and announcing, "Emergency landing!" Invariably this occurred over a pasture in which numerous cattle were grazing. After I maneuvered the plane through an acceptable approach, he would take over and proceed to hedge hop through the area, creating considerable consternation among the cattle.

Felt's Field was still unpaved at the time. It was designated as a civilian field, but a squadron of Army Air Force B-25s shared the facilities. There were several exciting occasions when a B-25 could not get its wheels down and it would come skidding in on its belly in the gravel. In most instances, little damage was done, and the plane would fly again.

Two friends and I traveled the 30 miles from Coeur d'Alene to Spokane for the Advanced CPT and for ground school, held at Gonzaga University. My primary means of transportation was riding the Auto Interurban Bus Line. Although my mother and Romey were divorced by that time, Romey still looked upon me with favor. As an employee of the bus line, he was able to arrange free passes for me for the daily trips to Spokane. Occasionally I would ride with Chuck Humphrey in his 1932 Ford V-8 coupe. I couldn't afford that very often because I was obligated to pay for part of the gasoline, and there was little cash to be had. Chuck subsequently joined the Navy as an aviation cadet and eventually flew torpedo bombers from small carriers in the Atlantic searching for German submarines.

Figure 2. Of the 600 WACO UPF-7s built, 140 are still registered.

As a high school athlete, Chuck was outstanding in track and a mainstay on the football team; however, when it came to his Navy physical examination the doctors discovered that

Chuck's heart was on the right side of his chest and all of the "plumbing" was the reverse of that in a so-called "normal" individual. There was a lot of soul searching and correspondence with the Bureau of Naval Personnel before they accepted him for active duty.

On completion of the secondary CPT course, I returned to school at the junior college, and at the same time began a serious attempt to join the military with the objective of becoming an aviator. Completion of the fall semester would qualify me scholastically by having completed two years of college. Still, physically, I had some problems.

Although the physicians had passed me for the primary and secondary CPT courses, they had ignored the fact that I was several pounds underweight. At age 20, I stood five feet nine and one-half inches tall and weighed about 125 pounds. Further, when it was really important that I pass the physical, I would become tense, and my blood pressure would exceed acceptable levels.

There followed six attempts to pass physical examinations as an aviation cadet—three for the Army Air Corps and three for the Navy. On those attempts to join the Army Air Corps, I had blood pressure and weight problems. On the third attempt, I passed both, but the flight surgeon looked at my deviated septum and loudly pronounced, "This man is disqualified. He will never be able to breathe properly at high altitudes!"

7 December 1941—The Japanese attack Pearl Harbor.

I had made alternate attempts to join the Navy, but again blood pressure and weight had been negative factors. The Navy, however, hadn't complained about my deviated septum. So, it was back to the Navy one more time with a resigned philosophy that if this did not work I would join the Air Force as a flight crewman. I wanted to fight the war.

Figure 3. The attack on Pearl Harbor galvanized the nation as never before.

In mid-March 1942, I found myself on an evening train, leaving Spokane, Washington, for Seattle to take one more physical examination. The Navy had sent me a round trip ticket, including an upper berth in a Pullman car and a check for $3.50 to cover the cost of meals enroute. Morning found us on schedule, passing over the Cascades and into Seattle's Union Station. It was only a seven or eight block walk up Second Avenue to 117 Marion Street and the Exchange Building where the Navy had its recruiting facilities.

The examination went well. A patient and understanding medical corpsman second class administered the Schneider test— a test where pulse rate and blood pressure are monitored while undergoing periods of exercise and rest. "Relax," he said. "No problem. Just stand there for a little while and I'll come back and check it." He did and the numbers he wrote down were within acceptable limits.

The eye examination and blood tests were conducted at a city clinic a few blocks from the Exchange Building. The drawing of blood was via a technique which resulted in a plain hollow needle being inserted into a vein with the draining blood being collected drop by drop in a waiting test tube. The procedure was somewhat disturbing since I was not accustomed to seeing flowing blood, particularly my own. Then, after having my eyes dilated and examined, I was turned out on the street without dark glasses on one of Seattle's few bright sunny days. With hands over my eyes, peering through slits between my fingers, I eventually found my way back to Marion Street.

By late morning, I was back at the Exchange Building and talking with the examining physician. He said I had passed everything except for my weight, which was 129 1/2 pounds. For my height, the requirements called for a minimum of 133 pounds. I asked for permission to come back after lunch for another weighing. After cautioning me about not making myself sick, he said, "Here, let me have that form." The understanding doctor erased the recorded weight and inserted 133 pounds. I had passed the physical exam!

Later that afternoon, I was sworn in as a Seaman 2nd Class V-5 which was the designation for individuals who would be entering the preliminary stage of flight training. One would be rewarded by being appointed Aviation Cadet after successfully completing the three months of preliminary training and would then proceed to Pensacola or Corpus Christi for final training. Orders to active duty were issued within a few weeks.

In the evening, I was back on the train, rolling toward Spokane. I remember the satisfaction of the day's events. And, as I lay there within the solid black confines of the upper berth, I found myself smiling with pleasure. Other events in my life have resulted in similar spontaneous smiles, but that was one of the sweetest.

About two weeks later, a letter arrived from the Navy informing me I would not go directly to flight training, but would be assigned to the first Pre-flight class at St. Mary's College in Moraga, California, reporting on 11 June 1942. The Pre-flight program consisted of three months of physical fitness and Navy indoctrination classes. Two other friends with whom I had flown in CPT were also being assigned to that class. Francis Smith, Bert Hudson, and I would all be reporting on the same date.

With nearly three months before reporting for active duty, I found employment with the U.S. Forest Service, planting Ponderosa Pine seedlings north of Coeur d'Alene, on a flat area adjacent to Rathdrum Prairie. After completing that project, we moved forty miles into the mountains of the Coeur d'Alene National Forest on the Little North Fork of the Coeur d'Alene River. There we planted Western White Pine in areas which had been burned or previously logged. We also worked on White Pine blister rust control, a disease which had serious adverse effects on White Pine forests.

April 17, 1942—Doolittle Attacks Tokyo

Figure 4. Lt Col. Jimmy Doolittle is the first to launch from the old USS Hornet (CV-8) on April 17, 1942 in the famous retaliatory raid against Japan.

In early June, I quit my Forest Service job and went back to town, anticipating receiving orders to active duty. When the letter arrived from the Navy, there were no orders; instead, there was a brief letter which stated that because I had been discharged from the National Guard due to a physical disability I would never be able to receive flight training in the Navy. Period!

Needless to say, that was a major disappointment. Rather than accepting their decision, I wrote back and presented my argument. My hernia had been corrected. I had passed the physical examinations for CPT and the Navy, and I had 80 hours of flight time, including completing a syllabus which was identical to the Navy's Primary Flight program. Their response was that my request was being forwarded to the Bureau of Naval Personnel in Washington D.C. for consideration.

June 5, 1942—Battle of Midway

Figure 5. Douglas SBD-3 "Dauntless" dive bombers of Scouting Squadron VS-8 from the original USS Hornet (CV-8) approaching the burning Japanese heavy cruiser Mikuma during the Battle of Midway, 6 June 1942.

June 11 came and went. My friends had received their orders and were on their way to St. Mary's for Pre-flight training. I was waiting. In the meantime, I got a job as a carpenter's helper during the early stages of the building of Farragut Naval Training Station, at the south end of Lake Pend Oreille, about 30 miles north of Coeur d'Alene. We were working 10 hours per day six days per week. I was apprehensive, waiting for a reply from the Navy. A rejection would find me enlisting in the Army Air Force as a flight crewman, or the draft board would find a place for me in the Army. I had a number of anxieties.

In their letter of 23 June 1942, the Navy advised me that the Bureau of Naval Personnel had approved my request, and that I would report directly to Sandpoint Naval Air Station, Seattle, Washington, Class 7B-42 on 16 July for flight training. Orders would follow. Ecstasy!!

The orders were received, and on 15 July 1942, wearing my $22.00 brown wool double breasted high school graduation suit, with double vents, I made ready for departure. My mother joined me for the trip from Coeur d'Alene to Spokane, where I would catch the train to Seattle.

On a beautiful summer day, with me carrying a small suitcase, anxiously looking forward to the coming events, we walked to downtown Coeur d'Alene and boarded the bus for Spokane. It was hard to believe, we were about three miles west of town when it suddenly occurred to me that my orders, train ticket, and meal chit were on the living room table back home. Stop the bus!!!

It was agreed that I would meet my mother in Spokane. I got off the bus, crossed the highway, and started to hitchhike back to Coeur d'Alene. The first car that came along stopped, picked me up, and the driver's route took me right past our house. The next problem—my mother had the house key. Solution: remove screen from the back bedroom window, open window, and climb in. It worked, but in doing so, I caught my trousers on a nail, in the window sill, which was used to secure the screen. Rip!!

With orders, train ticket and meal chit in hand, and a torn flap in the seat of my trousers, I was at the bus station in time to catch the next hourly bus for Spokane. The schedule still allowed adequate time before the train departed. Again, that night I was in a black upper berth. There was little sleep, however, with the sound of the wheels clicking rhythmically at each joint in the rails, the constant movement of the Pullman car, and contemplation of coming events.

I ate breakfast in the dining car as the train pulled over Snoqualmie Pass; by mid-morning we arrived at the station at Jackson and 5th Avenue. An electric city bus provided transportation over the hills of Seattle to the University district and then a transfer to a conventional bus took us the remaining distance to the Air Station, located on the shores of Lake Washington.

At the transfer point, I met another young man. Each of us had a few worldly belongings in a small suitcase and many uncertainties concerning the next events of the day. In conversation, we learned that we would be classmates in Class 7B-42. R. W. Hathaway, with square jaw and a beard of blue steel, and B. Bush with soft cheeks that had seldom seen a razor, were about to embark on a dramatic adventure!

Flight Training

On arrival at Sandpoint Naval Air Station, we were swept up in a whirlwind of activity! We reported to the student duty officer and officially became members of class 7B-42. Living quarters were assigned. We each got a dark green steel framed cot, two sheets, a pillow, and a white wool blanket with blue stripes across the top and bottom. The letters USN identified the blanket as property of the U.S. Navy. Nearby was a locker with color matching the bunks.

Our accommodations were in a large half-underground room which provided space for about fifty cadets. Windows at eye level on one side of the room revealed a narrow strip of well manicured grass and the base medical facilities across the street.

Following assignment of quarters, we were marched to the chow hall for lunch in our civilian clothes. Because of our lack of seniority, we marched behind the other cadets. Meals were served in the enlisted men's mess. Due to a demanding schedule, cadets were allowed to go to the head of the line. Cadets then alternately entered the chow line with the enlisted men. The "swabbies" disagreed with this arrangement; their comments to the cadets were frequently less than complimentary.

Monday morning, 17 July 1942—you are in the Navy now! First item of the day: issuance of uniforms. When that was over, nothing fit except shoes and socks. Strangely, we were issued Marine khakis as the work uniform. Shirts were coarsely woven; trousers had no back pockets; shoes were Navy issue black, a pair of oxfords, and a pair of high tops, both with the standard round toes. The shirt, size 16 collar and 33 inch sleeves more than met my 14 1/2 - 32 need. There was plenty of room around the neck, across the shoulders, around the chest and waist, and the cuffs kept the hands warm on cool mornings.

My dress blue trousers were created for someone with a 40 inch waist and inseam to match. The local tailor corrected that in short order, resulting in trousers that fit around the waist with the cuffs barely clearing the toes of the shoes. It made little difference that the back pockets were approximately one quarter of an inch apart, separated only by the inseam running from the center back down to the crotch. The fabric in the legs would have provided space for the largest thighs found on the most powerful running back of any professional football team.

Standard issue also included skivvies (white boxer shorts and round necked T-shirts), several pair of black socks, a khaki overseas cap, one black tie, a light poplin jacket, and a small white laundry bag. The waist of the boxer shorts was adjusted with side buttons and were of a fabric that refused to wear out.

With the issuance of our new uniforms, we would have no further use for our civilian clothes for the duration. Accordingly, we marched to the base post office and shipped our luggage, containing the clothes in which we had arrived the preceding day, off to the town from whence they had come. I subsequently learned that my mother gave away all of my civilian clothes. It was as though she was not anticipating my return—although she may have visualized my growing from a 129 lbs. weakling into a 175 lbs. athlete. That never happened.

It was standard Navy procedure to give every man a physical examination each time he reported to a new base. This was no exception. All of the cadets of Class 7B-42 joined a group of sailors and reported to sickbay for our physical examinations. Because of previous difficulties in passing a physical examination, I was very concerned. In a state of semi-nudity, I could feel perspiration flowing freely from my armpits. Would I pass???

It was a cursory exam by Navy corpsmen and there was no problem with the basic details. I was not, however, familiar with one aspect of the exam. We approached a corpsman who was seated and carefully observing each man's genital area. He spoke several syllables which issued forth as a single word "skinitbackandmilkitdown." For an innocent young man from a small lumbering town in North Idaho I was totally unfamiliar with the procedure. I was at a loss as to what he wanted. He was checking for infections caused by sexually transmitted diseases. Short arm inspection! No problem.

Then came the series of inoculations for a wide variety of possible illnesses. To simplify the procedure, each candidate removed his shirt, exposing both arms, and proceeded in a line between several corpsmen. Each began to work on the appropriate arm. Several shots were administered in a matter of moments. Next came the drawing of blood for further tests. I believe the young corpsman who was taking my blood had practiced only on an orange prior to attacking my arm. What a day!

We learned that for the first two weeks, one of our primary duties as "new" aviation cadets was to clean the heads. We became "Captains of the Head." This was a twice a day task. Ground school, calisthenics, close order drill, studies, and cleaning of quarters would fully occupy our time for the first four weeks. There would be no liberty during that period. Also, it was essential that each cadet maintain a high degree of personal cleanliness and keep his bed and locker "shipshape"! It was imperative that the foot of the bed have a satisfactory Navy tuck on each corner.

The training planes being used at NAS Sandpoint were bright yellow biplanes which had been built at the Naval Aircraft Factory in Philadelphia. The Navy designation was N3N, but they were commonly known as "Yellow Perils." Cadets, who had started their actual flight training, and their instructors, would fly from the air station to small outlying fields in the Seattle area to perform touch and go landings and basic maneuvers. Training flights to and from the air station frequently encountered traffic consisting of large patrol aircraft. This created hazards for both the trainers and the operational planes. There were PBY flying boats which would land on Lake Washington and subsequently be brought ashore at a ramp alongside the main runway. In addition, there were twin-engine land planes using the field. Both types of operational aircraft were being used for anti-sub patrol off the Pacific coast.

In a decision which was far beyond the comprehension of a lowly aviation cadet, plans had been made to move the training facilities to a new base on the east side of the Cascade Mountains. In late July, it was announced that we would be moving to the brand new Naval Reserve Auxiliary Air Station, Pasco, Washington. In 1942, Pasco was a town of approximately 8000 citizens, surrounded by little more than sand and sagebrush. It was located in south central Washington on the Columbia River at the south end of the "Big Bend." The river turns west at that point, and passes through the Columbia Gorge on its way to the Pacific Ocean.

Figure 6. The N3N Yellow Peril looked very much like the N2S.

It was early Sunday morning, 2 August 1942, that the cadet battalion, in dress blues, climbed aboard the grey Navy buses and was driven to the train station. It was a cool overcast morning in Seattle. The train ride over the mountains was enjoyable, but on arrival in Pasco in late afternoon, we knew there had been a dramatic change in climate. Temperatures were over 100 degrees, and humidity was at a skin shriveling level.

Our new home had sprouted from the sand and sage brush in the form of unfinished two story wooden boxes, similar to the barracks created for the soldiers of WW-I. They stood naked on concrete piers in a field of sand. There was a large newly paved asphalt mat, two spacious wooden hangars and a fleet of splendid new bright yellow Stearman bi-planes (N2Ss) parked in neat rows on the concrete ramp in front of the hangars.

Figure 7. Navy N2S

Essential structures had been completed which would be used for the administration building, sickbay, ship's service and the chow hall. There was also a swimming pool, surrounded by sand dunes, to be used for recreation and physical fitness training. Sidewalks had yet to be installed.

During the move, health records were lost, and it was necessary to repeat the series of inoculations and get another basic physical examination. There was ground school seven days a week with one half day of liberty on Sundays. The days started early and ended late.

The quality of food in the chow hall was poor. This was understandable, as the only individual who had had any experience in the galley was the chief petty officer in charge of the mess. The others were brand new recruits. There was one thing we could count on—pork and beans for breakfast on Wednesday and Sunday. The silverware was seldom clean, and the stainless steel trays invariably contained remnants of previous meals.

On 12 August, we received notice that the aviation cadets would no longer be seaman second class but "officially" aviation Cadets. Along with that benefit came a raise in pay from $32.00 to $75.00 per month. That was important, because I could then send enough money home to my mother for the $25.00 monthly payment on her house.

Four days later, I had my first flight with Ensign Haas as my instructor. The CPT flight training in Waco UPF-7s was beneficial in the Navy flight program; in only a short time, I soloed. The syllabus was basic. There were stalls, wingovers, chandelles, touch and go precision landings, and maneuvers to improve basic skills. There were no real acrobatics. Our flights took us aloft where we could view the "Big Bend" of the Columbia River to the north, and to the gorge leading the river through a massive cut in the Cascades to the west, and on to the Pacific Ocean.

Figure 8. Cadet Bush in a Navy N3N. Naval Auxiliary Air Station, Pasco, Washington October 12, 1942

It was exciting, challenging, satisfying. A learning experience gave us confidence and the belief that we would, without doubt, achieve our goal of becoming Naval Aviators.

The weather was hot, dry, and on occasion windy. On those days, the sand and large thorny tumble weeds drifted rapidly across the flight line, limiting the training activities of the neophyte aviators. Although the plane's engines were well protected with canvas covers, other parts of the airplanes were susceptible to the fine dust and sand. On more than one occasion, the planes were jacked up and wheels removed so brakes could be cleaned and bearings repacked to prevent damage when next put into service.

The days passed rapidly. Ground school was time consuming and the flight schedule proceeded at a steady pace. It was about that time, I became somewhat philosophical about the potential hazards of the course upon which we had embarked. In a diary notation on 10 September 1942 concerning the challenges of naval flight training I noted, "Even though the going is tough, someday we'll be damned glad and proud of the opportunities offered us. We don't think about the future. Some day some of us may be happy about it and some of us will regret it. It is a cinch that some of us will be killed before this mess is over."

22 September 1942—Ralph Wilson and his instructor were killed today at an outlying field southeast of the main station when their N2S spun in from about 500 feet. The plane caught fire on impact; it was gone in a matter of minutes.

In mid-September, the friends with whom I was originally scheduled to go to Pre-Flight School, Francis Smith and Bert Hudson, arrived to start their primary training. They had received orders to active duty five weeks before I had and now they were two months behind in the training program. They found that a bit annoying. I, however, was pleased to be near the end of the primary training and would soon depart for "The Annapolis of the Air."

My final check ride was passed 26 September, finishing the flight instruction at primary base. There would be some further ground training just to occupy time. Best of all, was a well deserved 48-hour liberty and the opportunity to return to Coeur d'Alene for a visit with special friends before going to

Pensacola. My sweetheart, and eventually my wife, Margie flew from Seattle to Spokane and Mother traveled from Denver. Romey was already in Spokane.

Liberty started at 1200 hours Saturday, 3 October. I crossed Highway 395 from the main gate and started hitchhiking to Spokane. It was not long before an elderly couple stopped and picked me up.

It took a long time for that trip. Because of a shortage of gasoline and tires, all travelers were to conserve those items by driving no faster than 35 miles per hour. Of course, those loyal and patriotic citizens adhered to the letter of the law.

I had two very delightful days in Coeur d'Alene! Indian summer was in its full glory. I spent some time with Mother and Romey as well as visiting friends. I went out to Margie's folks' house Saturday evening and did not get home until 0400 Sunday. Upon returning later that day, Marge and I spent most of the afternoon in the back yard wrapped in one another's arms. That evening we took Margie to Spokane to catch the train back to Seattle. Monday morning, I said farewell to Mother and Romey, caught a bus, and by noon was back at the base in Pasco. There were only six more days before we were to depart for Pensacola.

Activities during the next few days were directed primarily toward keeping us busy. There were ground school classes where we continued our studies of navigation, Morse code and blinker. The days passed uneventfully, and our departure from Naval Reserve Auxiliary Air Station, Pasco, Washington that Saturday evening, 10 October was rather subdued.

It was a cold October evening. Freezing weather had arrived in central Washington with a cold air mass that had blown in from the northern plains of Canada. Frost was evident on the dilapidated cracked concrete platform. Bare light bulbs hanging beneath the rusty chipped porcelain reflectors cast an inadequate glow on the platform and the twenty-five Naval

Aviation Cadets who were waiting to board their Pullman car and embark on a new and exciting adventure.

> Thy black cylindric body, golden-brass and silvery steel,
> Thy ponderous side-bars, parallel and connecting rods,
> > Gyrating; shuttling at thy sides,
> Thy metrical, now swelling pant and roar, now tapering
> > In the distance,
> Thy great protruding head-light fix'd in front,
> Thy long, pale, floating vapor-pennants, tinged with
> > Delicate purple,
> Thy knitted frame, thy springs and valves, the tremulous
> > Twinkle of thy wheels,
> Thy train of cars behind, obedient, merrily following —-

> Walt Whitman

Walt Whitman was not thinking of a monstrous Northern Pacific steam engine pausing temporarily in the Pasco, Washington train station when he described his locomotive. Still, the black cylindric body, the ponderous side-bars with their parallel and connecting rods, the pant, the great protruding headlight were all evident. Each intimate detail was revealed in the cold October night.

The train had just arrived from Seattle. Moments before, it had crossed the mighty Columbia River on a sturdy four-section cantilevered bridge, rolled through the western outskirts of Pasco, and stopped at the passenger station where we were waiting. The rear cars of the train were resting on the elderly overpass over Lewis Street which narrowed to nearly one-way traffic as it passed under the railroad tracks, reflecting an era when automobiles were small and few.

This Northern Pacific locomotive had wisps of steam leaking from its pistons. The resting engine was panting rhythmically, and a warm glow was issuing from the firebox. A narrow grey plume of smoke emerged quietly from the stack. The engineer, in his striped hat and overalls, long spouted oil can in hand, wended his way through the steam, oiling bearings and tending to his mechanical steed. The massive Baldwin 4-8-4 coal burner with drivers as tall as its master was pausing momentarily, waiting passively for impatient passengers to board before continuing on its way northeastward through the rolling hills of eastern Washington.

Figure 9. The Northern Pacific 4-8-4 coal fired Baldwin Locomotive similar to the one taking Aviation cadets to Pensacola, The Annapolis of the Air.

It was shortly after midnight, Sunday, 11 October 1942. We were in our winter uniforms (dress blues with caps to match), bags in hand, ready to climb aboard an ancient Pullman car that would be our home for the next five days. Destination— Naval Air Station Pensacola, Florida—the "Annapolis of the air."

A black skinned porter greeted us and pointed out the berths, made up along one side of the car, enough to meet the needs of our group. The other seats were to remain in an upright position for the entire journey. Sufficient current was being provided by the Pullman car's batteries to create a dull yellow glow in the light bulbs in their glass flower-like reflectors. They would be revitalized once the car was moving and the generators brought the batteries up to full charge.

In due course, the train rolled slowly out of the station into the darkness of the Palouse hills with their seemingly endless fields of newly planted winter wheat. The terrain northeast of Pasco had the appearance of huge ocean waves. They had been created in past centuries by deposition of loess, airborne dust, forming deep layers of fertile soil over large areas of eastern Washington and northern Idaho. The train track followed the path of least resistance, taking us through the troughs of those waves on a meandering journey toward Spokane, Washington.

Daylight found us in the Spokane rail yards, accompanied by the switching of cars and the making up of new trains. Parallel to the train tracks was Trent Avenue, the skid road of Spokane during the years of the "Great Depression." It was here, at the "Thin Dime Café" some friends and I, on an adventurous hitchhiking expedition to Spokane as young teenagers had a meal of stew and two slices of white bread with a slab of margarine for ten cents.

Now, our Pullman car was pushed, pulled, jerked, couplers thumped and clanged: air and steam hoses connected and in a short time, we were again headed through the flat Spokane valley toward the foothills of the Bitterroot Range into Northern Idaho.

I was looking at familiar terrain. This was home. Fifteen miles to the southeast, across a table flat Rathdrum Prairie, was Coeur d'Alene, Idaho, the small town in which I had lived since a young child. Off to the east was Mt. Canfield and to the north Mt. Rathdrum. They were landmarks that had much significance to me. I was aware, as the train rolled steadily on toward the Bitterroot Range and beyond, the experience which I was undergoing was the introduction to a new and vitally important chapter in my life. The eventual return to the community in which I had grown up, the friends, relatives, and life I had known for the past fifteen years would not be the same when I returned.

Sunday morning, 11 October, found us beyond the Spokane valley approaching Sandpoint, Idaho on Lake Pend

Oreille. The tracks took us around the north end of the lake and up the Clark Fork River. The river was turbulent at times, yet quiet, and peaceful at others, as it flowed through the heavily forested Bitterroot Range. There were brilliant splashes of gold on the mountain slopes where the Western Larch had turned color and were about to lose their needles for the winter season.

The next few days were a blurred memory. We crossed the Rockies and slowly worked our way across eastern Montana, Wyoming, South Dakota, the plains of the Mid-west, and on to St. Louis. Train traffic was heavy. Most trains were involved with troop movements or were freight trains carrying military equipment.

One train we were connected to contained several cars of WACs (Women's Auxiliary Corps). There was an instant attraction between some of the more adventurous members of our group and the young ladies. In the evening, the vestibules between the cars were crowded with scenes of attempted love making. However, it was all wishful thinking since the WAC officers were diligently patrolling the train to protect the morals of the young ladies in their custody.

In St. Louis, the steam engine pulled our train into the cavernous train sheds at the main station. Steam and smoke were trapped between the tracks and the half round roofs over the platforms. The roofs partially protected passengers from inclement weather. We stretched our legs by walking back and forth on the platform on that warm humid afternoon.

It was not long before we were rolling once more, across the Mississippi River into southern Illinois. It was evening, and as the train passed through numerous small communities we could see the local citizens sitting in their yards watching the trains roll by.

There were two more days of travel: rolling slowly, switching trains, waiting on sidings for other traffic to pass, Kentucky, Tennessee, Alabama and at last, Pensacola.

Pensacola

It was 1700 hours, 15 October 1942, Pensacola, Florida. Only residents of the "Gulf Coast" would recognize the weather conditions. A classical cold front had just passed through the area. A brilliant sun was still observable in the west, the sky was crystal clear, the breeze was out of the north, and humidity was low. The natives were pleased to see a change from the pattern of intense summer heat, southerly breezes, and high humidity.

Our dress blues with blue cap covers (winter uniforms) revealed that we were from a northern climate. Other arriving cadets were still in summer uniforms. It was almost as though our group belonged to a different navy. Confusion reigned. However, it was not long before Naval Air Station personnel took charge, organized us into platoons, and directed us to the ever present gray navy General Motors diesel buses. We climbed aboard with personal luggage. Foot lockers and suitcases were being loaded on trucks by enlisted personnel to be taken to our newly assigned quarters.

Again, there was the familiar whine of the automatic transmissions, the surge of shifting gears, black smoke pouring from the exhaust pipes, and the rumble of the diesel engines. We were entering the next phase of the great adventure!

My new home was Building 653—Room 1112. These were deluxe quarters compared to those at primary base. Two cadets were assigned to each room. There were two closets— one on each side of the room. Furniture consisted of two chests of drawers, a study table, and two chairs. Above a wash basin on the hallway wall were two medicine cabinets with mirrors. Two steel single cots, with bedding, occupied the corners of the room on the wall opposite the doorway. Two windows with roller type blinds allowed one a view of the barracks next door.

Cadets were expected to maintain the rooms in a state of cleanliness. Periodic "white glove" inspections were held, and woe be unto the cadet who failed to meet those rigid requirements. There was always the prospect of extra duty—an hour or so of marching with rifle in hand to compensate for the dereliction of duty. Each day the rooms were swept, dusted, and bunks carefully made up.

The first item on the schedule at our new base was the routine physical examination. It was passed with no difficulty. Blood pressure was 118/70 and the doctor suggested gaining some weight. Right! The dentist installed some fillings and placed red X marks on the chart indicating that all four wisdom teeth were to be removed. The Navy never got around to it. The teeth are still there more than 68years later.

The daily routine began at 0500 hours, with the shrill clanging of bells in the hallways, actuated by officers in charge of the cadets. All cadets gathered on the lawns in front of their respective buildings and went through a 15 minute period of calisthenics led by "90 day wonders"—officers who had completed three months of officer candidate school and before that had been athletes in college. Most of us accepted this experience with a bit of disdain and possibly a slight lack of respect for those in charge.

However, there were some innovative cadets in the corps. Roommates would take turns locking each other in their respective closets during the exercise period so they could get an additional 15 minutes of sleep. Officers who checked the rooms to insure all cadets were actively engaged in calisthenics invariably detected the culprits.

It was embarrassing for the cadets who participated in this activity and were found out. With an officer present, the cadet who had performed the morning calisthenics would return to the room and be required to unlock his roommate's closet, and reveal the culprit. Malingering! Extra duty! Both would participate in hours of marching with rifle in hand.

Breakfast was served about 0600 and activities of the day started by 0700. Newly arrived cadets went through an indoctrination program devoted exclusively to ground school for the first three weeks. Flight training began at week four when our days were split between the flight line and ground school.

26 October 1942—the aircraft carrier USS Hornet (CV-8) was sunk at the battle of Santa Cruz.

11 November 1942—Class 10-B-42-PC resumed flight training. We were transported via the large gray buses with the ever present diesel engines, the whining transmissions, and impatient cadets to Saufley Field. The aircraft now were the N3Ns rather than the Stearman. Profane, disagreeable, disgruntled, and difficult, Lt. (jg) J. A. Owens was my instructor.

The syllabus was identical to that in the secondary CPT program, and as a result, the primary training at Saufley Field was completed in an abbreviated period. All scheduled dual instruction periods were completed, but solo flights were limited. There were no problems completing the check rides. Thirty five hours of flying were managed in 18 days, to complete primary training. The primary phase ended with two hours of night flying—one hour with an instructor and one hour solo. This was my first night flying experience.

The instructor had to be a very brave soul. Saufley Field was a large black mat with a minimum of lighting. As one approached for a landing, it was like flying into a large black hole. The instructor remained with the cadet during several landings and the familiarization flight. At the end of the first hour, the instructor escaped and sent the cadet on his way for a solo flight. We both managed to survive.

Ground school and primary flight training had been completed. In early December, I moved from Mainside to Squadron Two at Ellyson Field for basic training. There, we flew SNV-1s (The Vultee Vibrator). It was a low wing monoplane with fixed landing gear, a two speed propeller (high and low pitch), and flaps.

This was the next step in a progression toward higher performance aircraft. We became familiar with the flying characteristics of a low wing monoplane and the additional mechanical features it provided. After being checked out, and acquiring a few solo hours, we began basic formation flying. A sense of urgency in moving the cadets through the program was apparent at Ellyson. I completed the basic training program in 15 days, despite frequently inclement weather.

In general, the atmosphere at Ellyson was austere. The quality of food was poor, and I was looking forward to getting back to Mainside and Squadron 3—instrument training. The basic-training flying experience was enjoyable and I increased my feeling of confidence as a pilot.

Figure 10. The Vultee SNV-1 'Valiant'. We called it the 'Vultee Vibrator'.

During the training at Ellyson, which all cadets received, we completed request forms, indicating the type of aircraft we would like to fly after receiving our "Navy Wings of Gold." The choices included fighters, dive bombers, torpedo planes, patrol planes, and observation planes. The student's choice would help determine the training he received in his final squadron at Pensacola.

I had given the matter a lot of thought. It was my opinion that under the right circumstances, I could inflict by far, the greatest damage to the enemy by flying dive bombers. Those views were presented with my request. On 13 December 1942, I was informed that my request had been approved and that I would receive dive bomber training in my final squadron.

It was back to the main base on 18 December for instrument training, but foul weather would delay further flying for almost two weeks. We had ground training classes, and got experience with the very crude flight simulators—the infamous Link Trainers. There was absolutely no similarity between flying a Link Trainer and modern simulators which fly exactly like an airplane. The Link did give one some experience in flying patterns on a simulated radio range, but it was a real battle to make that box respond in an appropriate manner.

Christmas Day at NAS Pensacola in 1942 brought a welcome change in the daily schedule. We had not had a day off for ten weeks. So, Christmas Day was especially enjoyed. There was a special dinner and in the evening a movie with Bing Crosby singing "White Christmas." Margie Ann, my girlfriend and future wife, sent me an elegant robe, which was never adequately used. It was my first Christmas away from home, but there was little nostalgia because of our busy schedule.

Figure 11. The Link trainer taught us how to fly safely in the clouds.

It was also at that time, I ordered $210.00 worth of uniforms. Dress blues, Navy greens (with two pairs of pants), and two sets of khakis—all of high quality. My view on the subject was, "Boy—they sure are expensive!" In addition, I purchased three sets of whites for a nominal fee from fellow cadets who were going into the Marines. At that point, one had to be optimistic that he would complete flight training.

Four days after Christmas 1942, I had my first instrument flight instruction. We were flying SNJ-4s, a low wing monoplane built by North American Aviation Co. It had retractable landing gear, hydraulic flaps and a constant speed propeller. The engine cowling was painted a bright red so other planes in the sky would be aware that the airplane was from the instrument squadron and was probably being flown on instruments. The instructor rode in the front seat and the cadet in back. A canvas hood was used to cover the cadet and isolate him from the outside world while he was performing his instrument training.

Figure 12. North American Aviation Company's SNJ-4 trainer.

Ordinarily, instruction did not begin until we were airborne, and at altitude. We frequently flew when there were low layers of clouds. The flight entailed climbing through the clouds, and then breaking into the clear. It was always exciting to climb through a grey oppressing environment, seeing the darkness gradually fading away, and then emerging into a clear blue sky with brilliant sunshine. The layer of snow white clouds stretched to the horizon, and one was in a world all of his own.

We would get under the hood and fly the radio ranges, learning to determine positions and practicing landing approaches. The instructor would go through unusual maneuvers and invariably give the student the controls when the airplane was on its back in a nose high attitude. It was the student's responsibility to recover, using only the needle/ball/airspeed technique. The needle/ball instrument tells the pilot if the aircraft is in a turn and if ailerons and rudder were coordinated. Gyros were caged (locked in position) before those maneuvers. Under normal circumstances, they would have "tumbled" and been of no use.

We also practiced instrument takeoffs. The cadet would taxi out to the runway and position the plane for takeoff. The artificial horizon would be adjusted, the directional gyro set and the check-off list completed. Down came the hood, and we were ready to go.

The next few minutes required diligent concentration as the cadet pushed the throttle forward to takeoff power. Then he'd watch the directional gyro to maintain heading; hold the stick lightly, letting the tail come up, maintain a slightly nose-high attitude by referring to the artificial horizon, airborne, wheels up, throttle back to climb power—scan the instruments continually to maintain proper attitude, climbing speed, and direction. The instrument squadron was an exhilarating experience!

In mid-January 1943, I moved to Bronson field, Squadron 4, for the final phase of flight training leading to graduation. Bronson field was located west of the main air station on Perdido Bay. Dive bombing training took place from the airfield. Adjacent to the airfield, on the shores of Perdido Bay, were hangars and ramps where future patrol plane pilots were trained in early versions of the PBY.

Our training during the next two months would be directed specifically toward dive bombing activities.. There would be 102 hours of flight time, mostly in SNJs, performing acrobatics, formation flying, gunnery, dive bombing, night flying and navigation flights.

Six of us flew together during our stay at Bronson Field. Hall Simons, Don O'Leary, and I had been in the same class at Pasco. In addition, there were Walt (Red) Jones, Norman Stehlick, and Bob Ricks. Three of us—Simons, Ricks and I— would eventually receive orders to Bombing Squadron -2.

Initially there was the "checking out" in the SNJ. We performed solo familiarization flights including touch-and-go landings, and a wide variety of acrobatics. We developed a feeling of confidence. We knew we were becoming aviators.

One experience still stands out in my memory. We were introduced to inverted spins shortly after arriving at Bronson Field. The objective was for the student to recognize an inverted spin and develop the skill to recover safely. Undue stress was placed on the aircraft during the maneuver, but the SNJ was not designed to withstand those stresses. Instead, we performed the spin in a Stearman (N2S) Yellow Peril. The instructor positioned himself in the front cockpit and the cadet was relegated to the back seat.

When an acceptable altitude was reached, and the sky was clear, the instructor demonstrated the maneuver. Roll the aircraft onto its back, power off, push the stick all the way forward to raise the nose above the horizon, and when the plane stalled, apply full left rudder. The plane immediately went into a violent spin.

The applied forces were the reverse of that normally experienced in a spin. If seat belts had not been fastened, the occupants would have been ejected and had the opportunity to test their parachutes. Dust and dirt particles were removed from the belly and floor panels of the airplane, filling the cockpits. It was like a cyclone!

Recovery was essentially the reverse of recovering from a "normal" spin. The stick was brought back, dropping the nose to increase flying speed, and rudder pedals were positioned to control directional stability. Full recovery was achieved by rolling the plane back to an upright position and establishing stable speed and attitude. Next, it was the student's turn.

During our stay at Bronson, some accidents resulted in casualties in flights other than our own. Those casualties did not have the significance that they would have had if the persons involved were close friends. The events were remote, and did not have a personal effect on our immediate activities.

We did have a close call one day when Don O'Leary tried to take off with the carburetor heat in the "on" position. Hot air flowing into the carburetor was not adequate to provide the necessary power for takeoff. He did not get off the ground. Instead, Don ran off the end of the runway, knocked down a quarter mile of chain link fence, bounced across a road, and broke off a half dozen tall, skinny Southern Pine trees about three feet above the ground. Fortunately, the plane did not burn, and Don, being securely fastened with shoulder and lap belts, was not scratched. They didn't wash him out either.

Navigation and dive bombing flights were conducted in OS2U Kingfishers (built by Consolidated Aircraft Co.) adapted for land use. This airplane was normally configured with a large single float under the fuselage and a float at each wing tip. It was designed as an observation aircraft and flew from battleships and cruisers. The planes were launched from catapults when used in the fleet. Recovery was made by landing to the lee of the mother ship and then being hoisted aboard. In a land configuration, the OS2U had fixed landing gear and was an awkward looking plane. However, it was sturdy and could withstand the stress of steep dives when used for the dive bombing phase of training. In addition, it had adequate range to permit long navigation flights over the Gulf of Mexico.

On navigation flights, our group would be divided into two sections of three planes each. We would start at the same position and fly opposite courses using dead reckoning. Each cadet would lead one leg on a triangle course which would take us out over the Gulf about 100 miles. One of the objectives was for the two sections to rendezvous at the half way point in the flight. We were successful on every occasion. All of the flights were monitored by our instructors who accompanied us to insure we did not get lost and that we really did perform satisfactorily.

Gunnery was an exciting part of the training. We flew SNJs with one .30 caliber machine gun in. The target was a white cotton sleeve about three feet in diameter and about 15 feet long. It was towed at the end of a long cable by one of the fellow cadets in another SNJ. Gunnery was conducted over the Gulf in designated areas where surface traffic was prohibited.

**Figure 13. The Vought OS2U Kingfisher with fixed gear
rather than floats. Used by Aviation cadets in their final
training squadron for dive bombing and navigation flights.
February 1943.**

The procedure called for positioning one's self ahead,
above and to one side of the tow plane. The gunnery run was
started with a 180 degree turn toward the tow plane, keeping it in
sight at all times. At that point, we would be flying in the
opposite direction to the tow plane.

At the appropriate moment, we would roll the plane over
in a steep dive, picking up the target in the gun sight,
establishing the proper lead, and firing as we dove past the
sleeve. It was inappropriate to make a run which found one
chasing the sleeve in a flat position with .30 caliber bullets being
directed toward the tow plane.

This was a period of training that was far more relaxing
than previous instruction. Activities were directed primarily
toward flying rather than ground school, drilling and athletics.
There was much more free time, liberty was available every
evening and we had one day off every week. Instructors treated
the cadets as human beings—almost like fellow officers.

When training was completed on 12 March 1943, we were transferred to the main base in preparation for receiving our commissions and Navy Wings of Gold. Those impressive events took place on 16 March.

It was a beautiful morning. There had been a classical cold frontal passage during the night, similar to that day five months before, when we arrived in Pensacola. The breeze was out of the north, temperatures were cool, and there wasn't a cloud in the brilliant blue sky. We had assembled in formation on the concrete ramp in front of the Administration Building and Rear Admiral G. D. Murray, USN, presented us with our commissions and our Wings of Gold. It was a proud moment!

No time was wasted that day. Following graduation ceremonies, we reported to the duty officer to pick up our orders for further training. We were issued $150.00 for uniform allowance, and then checked out of the various departments on the base. I was given orders to pre-operational training at NAS, Miami, Florida.

Figure 14. On March 16, 1943, Ensign Billy Bush received his Navy "Wings of Gold."

United States Naval Air Station

Pensacola, Florida

Know all men by these presents that

Ensign Billy Bush, A-B(N), U. S. Naval Reserve

has completed the prescribed course of training and having met successfully the requirements of the course has been designated a

Naval Aviator

In Witness Whereof, this certificate has been signed on this 16th day of March 1943, and the Seal of the Naval Air Station hereunto affixed

Commander, U. S. Navy
Superintendent of Aviation Training

Rear Admiral, U. S. Navy
Commandant
Naval Air Training Center

Figure 15. Billy Bush's Certificate of graduation as a Naval Aviator - March 16, 1942

Pre-Operational Training

At 1900, 16 March 1943, I was on a train bound for Jacksonville. There was a change of trains there and then on to Miami. I was joined by a fellow classmate from primary training, Walt Ottmer, who had joined the Marines, but was also going to Miami for further training in preparation for flying dive bombers.

Our orders allowed two days' delay in reporting to Miami. We stopped in Daytona Beach for two days of relaxation. We arrived in Miami 21 March, anxious to proceed with additional training before being assigned to an operational squadron.

Miami was a new experience! We were now officers and had new freedoms which far exceeded those as cadets. Our quarters were the same as at Pensacola. However, there was no longer the rigid schedule nor the demanding ground school activities. There was, of course, the usual checking in, the physical examination and the assignment to a flight group.

Most of the flight members from Bronson Field arrived, and we were assigned to the same flight group in Miami. There was Bob Ricks, Hall Simon, Don O'Leary, Walt Jones, and I. A new member, Jim McGee, also joined the flight. We would all be flying together for the next two months, and three of us would subsequently fly together during the next year and a half as members of Bombing Squadron Two.

After several familiarization flights in SNJ's, we were introduced to our first operational type carrier aircraft—BT-1s, predecessors to the SBD Douglas Dauntless dive bomber. The BT-1 was originally designed and built by Northrop Corp. However, Northrop was bought out by Donald Douglas in 1938. With a change of paint and a number of modifications, the BT-1 became the SBD.

Figure 16. Northrop BT-1, predecessor of the famous SBD

Our BT-1s had semi-retractable landing gear, a wing span of almost 42 feet and a length of 32 feet. They were powered by Wright XR-1820-32 engines with a rating of 1000 HP takeoff power. Maximum speed was 265 mph and cruise speed was 155 mph. Perforated split flaps provided excellent dive-bombing characteristics. The use of the bomb sight, similar to a two foot long telescope, required the use of a special technique when going into a dive-bombing attack.

The BTs were well used. Their engines leaked a lot of oil and the windshields always had a film on them, restricting visibility. We carried grease rags on every flight and would reach out into the slipstream and wipe the windshields as clean as possible before starting the dive.

Each flight took off individually, rendezvoused, and flew as a formation to the bombing range in the Florida swamps near Lake Okeechobee. The target consisted of a large white circle with smaller circles inside and a bull's eye in the center.

After attaining the proper altitude, the flight leader would approach the target and the attack would begin. The leader started his dive, with each member of the formation following in sequence, each attacking the target from a slightly different angle. The group rendezvoused again with a different member of the group taking the lead. During every flight, each member would have the responsibility of leading the group through one attack.

We would maneuver the plane into the attack position, view the target by sighting parallel to the bomb sight, and then place one eye to the sight. The cross hairs were set on the target. The plane would be flown through the dive, and at the appropriate moment, we released our small practice bombs.

It was not practical to use conventional sized bombs for training purposes. In those instances, we carried a six compartment pod under the wing. Each compartment accommodated a cast iron practice bomb approximately eight inches in length with a black powder shotgun shell in the nose. On impact, the shell would explode, with a resulting cloud of dense black smoke, by which the accuracy of the attack could be determined. A bomb was released each time the release lever in the cockpit was pulled. It was possible for a pilot to go through six dive-bombing attacks on each flight.

We also flew another carrier type aircraft which dated back to the 1930s, the original Curtiss Helldiver. This airplane became well known when the movie "Helldiver" was produced, starring Robert Taylor. The movie portrayed, of course, a glamorous Naval Aviator flying dive bombers from aircraft carriers.

This Helldiver, designated as SBC (Scout Bomber Curtiss), was an outdated aircraft that had many deficiencies. It was an underpowered bi-plane with accessories that were all manually operated. The wheels were retracted into the fuselage by using a hand crank on the right side of the cockpit. A bicycle type chain ran through the cockpit floor into the belly and, through a system of gears, actuated the landing gear.

Figure 17. The early version of the Curtiss SBC Helldiver. Obsolete in the fleet but used by new Naval Aviators in "pre-operational" before joining a squadron (1943).

When extending the landing gear, one had to exercise extreme caution that the wheels were not allowed to drop rapidly. If the pilot lost control of the landing gear handle, gravity would result in a rapid lowering of the gear, an uncontrolled spinning of the handle in the cockpit, and possible fractures of bones in the pilot's right hand.

Because of the landing gear's narrow wheel base, an unstable condition occurred during landing. In addition, the brakes were inadequate, and between the two conditions, aircraft frequently left the runway and careened, out of control, across the Florida sand.

Manually operated flaps were located on the lower wing and could be used in two configurations, one for landing, and the other for dive-bombing. When in a dive bombing attack, the flaps would be "split," acting as a brake. Even with the split flaps, the SBC would drop through the sky as if there was no restriction.

Fortunately, experience in the SBCs was limited to familiarization and navigation flights. The navigation flights took us over the Bahamas and the Florida Keys. On those flights over the Keys south of Miami, it was not unusual to find ourselves deliberately only inches above the water with miniature water spouts being drawn into the slipstream of the propellers.

Now we had time for more instrument training in the SNJ's and for the beginning of field carrier landing practice. It would not be long before we would be performing the "actual" carrier landings. When we left Miami, we were to be fully qualified for the next major step in progressing to the fleet.

The two months in Miami were enjoyable. The weather at that time of the year was delightful. We had few responsibilities other than flying. There were the athletic activities of volley ball, swimming, and sun bathing. We acquired "healthy" sun tans by lounging at the swimming pools.

Liberty in Miami will be a period long remembered. There were the visits to town in our freshly starched whites. We rode the city buses to town but didn't sit down for fear of wrinkling our trousers. It was youth in all of its confidence and innocence—beautiful specimens—dark "healthy" tans—heavily starched, neatly pressed white uniforms with ensign epaulets and Navy Wings of Gold. There were visits to the night clubs on Miami Beach and other entertainment spots. Little thought was given to the future. Enjoy today!

In the spring of 1943, with WW-2 the primary focus of activities, Miami still had its small entrepreneurs. There were many one man orange juice stands on the streets. Fresh squeezed orange juice! Before your eyes, the orange was sliced, with the halves in their turn being placed on the squeezing mechanism. The lever brought swiftly down—juice and pulp flowing into the glass. Refreshing!!

It was a period in life never to be forgotten. Music to be remembered—Ella Fitzgerald singing "That Old Black Magic Has Me in its Spell," and that favorite song "When they Begin the Beguine." Even today, the memories are still vividly impressed on my mind.

Pre-operational training was completed on 22 May 1943, and orders were received to Air Atlantic Fleet, Norfolk, Virginia via Glenview NAS in Illinois. I was to report to the Commander Carrier Qualification Training Unit, Glenview NAS prior to midnight 24 May. Fifteen days' delay was allowed, to count as leave, before arriving in Norfolk.

I left Miami, coach class, straight through to Chicago on a fast diesel engine "streamliner" at 1725 hours on 22 May. It was a forty eight hour trip on semi-reclineable seats—then, on to Glenview Naval Air Station. It was a comfortable train. Passengers were mostly military. There was a lot of camaraderie and singing of patriotic songs. The train became quiet as the evening progressed—lights dimmed—passengers dozed and slept. For 1943, it was a fast trip on a deluxe train.

At Chicago, we had to transfer from one train station to another. I arrived at Glenview NAS in the early afternoon of 24 May. There was some delay in scheduling more field carrier landing practice, and the actual carrier landings.

It may sound rather unusual to talk about carrier landings and Glenview NAS, Illinois, in the same breath. However, the Navy had acquisitioned two large "cruise ships" on Lake Michigan, removed the superstructure, and converted them to small carriers. There weren't any German submarines operating in Lake Michigan. The carriers were christened "USS Sable" and "USS Wolverine."

Figure 18. USS Wolverine on Lake Michigan 29 May 1943. The author qualified aboard this ship by making eight carrier landings.

On 28 May 1943, I spent a little more than an hour doing field carrier landing practice, and on 29 May qualified aboard the USS Wolverine with eight landings. As with many new challenges, there was a certain amount of apprehension. And, rightly so. My carrier qualification experience was not entirely trouble free: I remember with some chagrin that first landing. In eagerness to get on the deck and catch a wire, I "dove for the deck." Embarrassment!! The landing was successful, but two tires were blown out. There was room on the starboard side of the deck, forward of the island, where I taxied the SNJ on those poor flopping tires. I had to wait below deck while the tires were changed. The next seven landings were uneventful.

In later years while reviewing log books, I realized that the field carrier landing practice fell on my 23rd birthday, followed one day later with carrier qualifications. Birthdays did not occupy a position of importance under those circumstances.

On 30 May, I checked out of NAS Glenview with orders to report to NAS Norfolk with 15 days delay (to be counted as leave). It was off to Coeur d'Alene, Idaho, for a reunion with Margie Ann. The Northwest DC-3 "hopped" all the way to Spokane, Washington. It was more than an all-night flight!

On arrival in Coeur d'Alene, I found that Margie had left a short time before to become a WAF (Women's Auxiliary Air Force) pilot in Sweetwater, Texas. Disappointment!! The next two weeks were spent visiting friends. Then it was aboard another Northwest Airlines DC-3, "hopping" to Chicago. There was an overnight, and then on to Norfolk, Virginia, on 15 June.

Civilian planes were using NAS Norfolk for operations. When we landed, we were escorted aboard a school bus with blacked out windows, to the main gate. Passengers were not supposed to see what was going on within the confines of the air station. When we got to the main gate, those who were reporting to the base got off, boarded a Navy bus, and made our way back to the Administration building to report for duty.

It was several days before orders were issued. During that time, Jim McGee arrived. We both subsequently received orders to report to Bombing Squadron 14, NAS, Cape May, New Jersey.

On the evening of 21 June, both Jim and I left Norfolk and headed for New Jersey. Allowance for this journey was $28.19. We boarded a ferry at Norfolk, crossed Chesapeake Bay, and then caught a train to Philadelphia. In the early morning, we transferred from one train to another in Philadelphia, and then it was on to Cape May.

Late in the afternoon of 22 June, we arrived at the train station in Cape May. What a reception!! This was vacation land for the folks on the East Coast when they went to "the shore." There were many horse-drawn surreys with the fringe on the top, where hotel employees were hawking the hotels for which they worked. Hop aboard, and the drivers would take you to their destination.

When we took a taxi out to NAS Cape May, we found that it was a blimp base. We were further ordered to NAS Wildwood, a new base in the New Jersey swamps half-way between Cape May and Wildwood. There we would become members of Bombing Squadron 14—subsequently to become Bombing Squadron -2.

Squadron Training

It was a varied group of Naval Aviators who gathered at NAS Wildwood in June, 1943 for the formation of Bombing Squadron-2 (VB-2). Our squadron was the dive bombing portion of Air Group-2 which was composed of dive bombing, torpedo, and fighter squadrons. While we were to conduct our initial training at Wildwood, the torpedo (VT-2) and fighter (VF-2) squadrons would be training at Naval Air Stations in Quonset Point, Rhode Island, and Atlantic City, New Jersey.

Bombing Squadron Two was composed of only one proven combat pilot. Most of us had just finished flight training and had received some pre-operational training. Vernon Micheel, a holder of the Navy Cross, had participated in the Battle of Midway. Hal Buell had seen active duty in the South Pacific but, in reality, had seen little actual combat.

Jesse W. Bamber, who was older than most of us, had gone through training as an enlisted man before the war, and had been designated an Aviation Pilot (AP). His previous experience had been as a flying Chief Petty Officer, co-pilot in a PBY patrol squadron. He was a truly dedicated "regular" Navy man. Instead of being designated as U.S. Naval Reserve, Jesse was United States Navy—USN! As such, he became known as Jesse W. Bamber, USN. He was given a temporary commission early in the war. Jesse would experience more than the average life threatening experiences during the next year and a half. Most of us were newly commissioned officers and newly designated Naval Aviators. Of our flight group in Miami, Jim McGee, Bob Ricks, Hall Simons, and I received orders to Bombing Squadron Two.

Our new squadron was commanded by Lieutenant Commander G. B. (Soupy) Campbell USN. Soupy was an Academy man and had only recently gone through flight training. On graduation, as a full lieutenant, he had been assigned as executive officer of the Observation and Scouting Training Squadron at Pensacola.

It was in the Observation and Scouting Squadron that a small number of cadets were trained as pilots to fly the single engine float planes that were carried on cruisers and battleships. Prior to the rapid development of aircraft carriers, the scouting planes were used as "the eyes of the fleet." They would be catapulted from the ship, search out the enemy and act as spotters to assist in gunnery fire control.

Figure 19. An OS2U Kinfisher seaplane being placed on the aft catapult of the USS Missouri.

When it came time to recover the scouting plane, the ship was brought to a halt. The pilot would land in calm waters in the lee of the ship and be hoisted aboard. Those procedures were made obsolete with the incorporation of aircraft carriers in the fleet, and pilots on the battleships and cruisers got very little flight time.

When "Soupy" was promoted to Lieutenant Commander, he was given command of Bombing Squadron-2. At that time, he had little more flying experience, and in some cases much less, than the other members of the newly formed squadron. His credentials consisted of being an Academy man and having had several years of Navy experience.

Lieutenant Russell Lord was the executive officer. Russ would be with the squadron until we were sent overseas. Just before going aboard ship, he was promoted to Lieutenant Commander and was given command of a land based dive bombing squadron in the Solomon Islands area.

Lieutenant J. R. (Smitty) Smith was Operations Officer. Smitty was not a particularly memorable individual. He was portly—almost fat—and had achieved his position through seniority. Smitty remained with the squadron throughout our tour of sea duty and return to the U.S.

Two days after reporting for duty at NAS Wildwood, we started familiarization flights. We were flying the latest models of the Douglas Dauntless dive bombers, SBD-5s. They were low wing monoplanes with a wing span of about 42 feet and a length of about 33 feet. Their loaded weight was about 11,000 pounds. A Wright R-1820-60 Cyclone engine provided 1200 hp takeoff power, turning a three blade constant speed Hamilton Standard hydromatically controlled propeller. Armament consisted of two .50 caliber machine guns firing forward through the propeller arc and two .30 caliber machine guns (flexible) controlled by the radioman, firing from the back cockpit. The wings did not fold for carrier operations.

The bomb sights on the SBDs were a vast improvement over the BTs. They consisted of a heavy piece of plate glass positioned at a 45 degree angle above a light source. That light source projected an orange colored bull's eye, with cross hairs, on the glass. One could sit in the cockpit and view a scene which incorporated more than 180 degrees, and yet see the target which would be clearly outlined by the bomb sight.

Figure 20. The Douglas SBD, hero of the Battle of Midway.

A variety of bombs could be carried by the SBD, but it was limited to a maximum of 1600 pounds. All bombs were attached to external racks. When the main bomb was released, a yoke would direct it away from the belly of the aircraft and prevent it from dropping through the propeller arc. Small bombs could be carried under the wings, and released independently of the larger bomb carried under the belly. Cruising speed of the SBD was about 150 knots and specifications defined its range as about 1500 miles. In reality, the range was much less than that.

The SBD engine did not have an electric starter. Instead, the plane captain (mechanic) would take a heavy crank with a handle that would accept two hands, and had a lever arm of about one foot, insert it through an opening in the cowling, and start cranking an inertia fly wheel. When the inertia starter was up to speed—one could tell by the high pitched whining sound—the plane captain would stand clear, give a "thumbs up," and the pilot would engage the starting gears. The plane captain was very disappointed if the pilot did not get the engine started on the first try.

In my initial check out flight, the SBD demonstrated little difference in flight characteristics from the BT-1 which we had flown in Miami. The next few days found us involved with intensive training which continued during our stay at NAS Wildwood. There were up to three flights a day when we did gunnery, formation work, and practice dive bombing.

In July, I had my first flight with Jack Secrest, radioman 3rd class, who would eventually become my permanent rear seat man. He had just turned 18 years old, was six feet tall, and weighed about 175 pounds. He was strong enough to handle capably the twin .30 caliber machine guns in the back seat. Those guns were to help protect us from attacking enemy fighters.

Jack, from Monroe, North Carolina, spoke with a characteristic southern drawl. We later developed into a dedicated team as we shared experiences ranging from routine to life threatening.

Training activities filled our three months at NAS Wildwood. Dive bombing attacks on moving targets were an important part of that training. Those moving targets were PT boats with armored topsides, which would be stationed off the New Jersey shore, waiting for the dive bombers.

Our bombing attacks would be coordinated with the target boat via radio. At the appropriate moment, we would start our dives and the PT boat would perform evasive maneuvers. We were using the small practice bombs with the black powder shotgun shells—six bombs each in the pod under the right wing, allowing six dive bombing runs. It was a challenge to hit that small moving target but we did on occasion. What was it like to be in the target boat when those small bombs hit topside?

Figure 21. My gunner Jack Secrest near the end our tour in September 1944—Western Pacific.

At the end of our training flights, we usually ended in an exhilarating "tail chase." Although our SBD's were not designed as fighters, they could still perform all of the stressful maneuvers required of a fighter. We would start at a high altitude, six planes, one behind another. There would be loops, slow rolls, snap rolls, and chandelles. Near the end of the chase we would be stepped down one behind another flying only a few feet above the wetlands of southern New Jersey. Those events were not part of the training program. They were extemporaneous!

Instrument flight training continued in SNJs. The pilot receiving the training was again in the back seat with a hood over the cockpit. A fellow pilot in front carefully observed the sky for other air traffic.

We alternated positions so that everyone received his allotted training. It was during this phase of training that I flew with "Tex" Hardin. "Tex," of course, was from Texas. He was a year or so older than I. He had completed flight training about a year before and was a Lieutenant Junior Grade (jg). "Tex" would become the squadron's first combat casualty on 30 March 1944.

Further expanding our flight experiences, we had gunnery practice where we attacked a towed sleeve. There was night flying in murky skies over the Atlantic. In mid-August, we began field carrier landing practice. When the landing signal officer was satisfied with our performance, we flew to Norfolk and qualified on a small jeep carrier built by the Kaiser ship yards. Those ships were commonly referred to as "Kaiser Coffins."

The exercise was performed on Chesapeake Bay, which was almost like having one's own private ocean. The mouth of the bay was closed off with anti-submarine nets, eliminating the danger of submarine attack while conducting flight operations. In open waters (the Atlantic Ocean), the ship would be vulnerable to submarine attack, as it steamed into the wind on the steady course necessary during carrier qualifications.

Although we considered ourselves increasingly proficient in the art of flying, lapses occurred occasionally. There were actually three "wheels up" landings, on different occasions, when the pilots neglected to use their landing check off lists. Gene Tull did it twice. Embarrassing!!! Those incidents were recorded in their flight records, but no disciplinary action was taken.

The summer of 1943 was not all work. We had some social activities. Cape May and Wildwood, prior to the war, were vacation spots for many people in the New York City and Philadelphia areas. The war did not change that. There were the large Victorian hotels of wooden construction, with elaborate ginger bread trimmings. Those hotels were filled with the many vacationers from the large cities.

Figure 22. The Hornet tying up to the mooring at Fox 9 Ford Island, Pearl Harbor March 4, 1944. Air Group 15 is on the flight deck. Photo taken from Essex (CV-9) who would soon take Air Group 15 aboard while Hornet would take Air Group 2 into her first combat with the Japanese.

Cape May had a boardwalk similar to the one in Atlantic City. It ran parallel to the beach from the south side of Cape May to the north side. A galvanized pipe railing was installed on the beach side of the walk. At regular intervals, steps led from the board walk down to the sandy beach. The steps would accommodate swimmers and those just wanting to lie in the sun. Adjacent to the beach were facilities where one could rent a small closet-like dressing room for the day for changing clothes and securing valuables while on the beach.

There were the usual food stands, salt water taffy shops, restaurants, and bars. One of the more prosperous bars had live entertainment—two piano players, each with his own grand piano, on an elevated platform, playing their own routines as well as songs requested by the customers.

Cape May was primarily a Navy town with personnel from the local blimp base, NAS Cape May. In addition, there were the many civilians on vacation. Most of the people had no sense of urgency. The thought of war was far away. "I'm Going to Buy a Paper Doll to Call My Own," sung by the Mills Brothers was the hit song of the summer.

Wildwood was similar to Cape May, but it also had a theme park in conjunction with the board walk. It boasted a roller coaster, Ferris Wheel, and similar carnival type attractions. It was not unusual for some of the members of the squadron to "thrill" the spectators by buzzing the theme park and performing dramatic maneuvers. Wildwood was where the action was. Cape May was for the more reserved. Perhaps that was why Jim McGee and I usually went to Cape May.

We could take Navy transportation from the air station to both Cape May and Wildwood. Sometimes, however, we would hitchhike to town when on liberty. It was on one of those occasions that Jim and I encountered a lima bean machine that was in operation alongside the road. The bean plants had all been freshly harvested and were stacked in a big pile. The operator was using a pitch fork to throw them into a large hopper at one end of the machine. At the other end, a continuous stream of beans appeared, and the empty pods and plants were disgorged to the side.

Flying over the menhaden processing plant, located on the shore just north of Cape May, was another unusual experience. Local fishermen would fish offshore, netting tons of the small bony fish. The fish were brought to the processing plant and converted to fish meal for cattle feed and fertilizer. Although we did not see the plant from the ground, we did have an olfactory experience from several thousand feet in the air as we flew over it. Most impressive!

For an adventurous extrovert, Cape May and Wildwood were ideal for attracting female companionship. However, as a reserved young man with church-taught moral values learned as a teenager, I ruled that out. There was no carousing, no smoking, and no consumption of alcohol. Jim McGee shared those values, but we were in the minority in the squadron.

The summer activities continued at a high level through Labor Day. The following day, however, there was not a soul to be seen on the beach or the boardwalk, even though the weather continued fair and inviting. The season had ended. Two weeks later, we too were gone. It was on to NAS Quonset Point, Rhode Island where we would rendezvous with our torpedo and fighter squadrons to complete our air group training—one more step on our way to the fleet, and combat.

It was at that point where excess personnel were eliminated from the squadron roster because of perceived inadequacies in flying skill or personality conflicts.. Hall Simons was one of those who received orders back to NAS Norfolk. He subsequently was transferred to a utility squadron operating out of Panama and remained there for the duration of the war.

**Figure 23. Vertigo the Wolf, Bombing Squadron Two's
mascot, with all member's signatures**.

Quonset Point

NAS Quonset Point was located about 15 miles south of
Providence on the west side of Narragansett Bay. It was a well
established base with attractive brick buildings, well maintained
lawns and beautiful maple trees. The airfield was bordered on
three sides by Narragansett Bay and was used for transport, anti-
submarine and carrier group activities.

The air group's objective was for the three squadrons to
learn to fly in the same sky as a coordinated group. The dive
bombers led the way with the torpedo squadron stepped down
and slightly behind. Fighters were stationed above, slightly

ahead, and to either side of the main group. Since the fighters were faster than either the dive bombers or the torpedo planes, they would cover the group by flying a scissor pattern from side to side. This permitted them to maintain the proper defensive position, and at the same time, fly at a speed which would permit engagement on equal terms if attacked by the enemy.

Flying formation with a six or twelve plane formation requires skill. Flying formation with twelve dive bombers, eight torpedo planes, and a dozen fighters—all in a compact group—requires even greater discipline, skill, and strict attention to the task at hand. For obvious reasons, those flights were referred to as "group gropes." We improved greatly with time.

One of our night flying "group gropes" was an experience to remember! It took place on a night when there was no moon and we were over Long Island Sound with no horizon or lights for orientation. It was like flying in a large black box. It was imperative that we maintained proper position on our section leader, and he in turn, had to maintain proper position on the division leader. Each individual had to exercise the utmost discipline to insure completing a successful flight. We did it—but I can still remember the sensation of vertigo which prevailed, even though an occasional quick glance at the gyro and artificial horizon would confirm we were flying straight and level.

Night field carrier landing practice was in the same category. A simulated carrier deck was established at the south end of the runway with the landing signal officer at the aft port side position. We made our approaches over Narragansett Bay at an altitude barely above the water and at speeds slightly above stalling.

From a downwind position, the plane was flown in a gentle 180 degree left hand turn toward the simulated carrier

Figure 24 Pilots of Bombing Squadron Two—Quounset Point Rhode Island, October 1943.

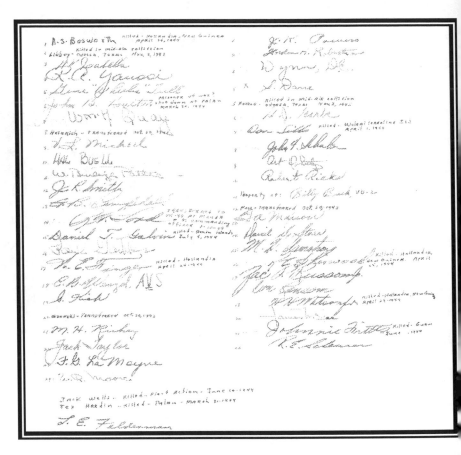

Figure 25. Autographs of all the members of Bombing Squadron Two

deck. The landing signal officer would use his battery powered electric wands to help guide us in our approach. We would attempt to make any necessary corrections as directed. If an acceptable approach was achieved, we would level our wings as we came over the carrier deck. Cut! Drop the nose, tail down— touch, and go! Then, around for another approach. If we got a "wave off," it was full throttle, slowly gain altitude, and come around for the next try.

Night field carrier landing practice is dangerous under the best of circumstances. When flying propeller driven aircraft, with high powered engines that deliver a lot of torque, one is in a particularly hazardous position. At a slow speed, with the engine at full power, and the propeller rotating in a clockwise direction, torque tends to cause the left wing to drop and it is necessary to apply a lot of top rudder to maintain the proper attitude. The aircraft is in a nose high position, with restricted visibility, and speed is barely above stalling. There is little room for error.

It was October 1943 and New England colors were at their best. The maple trees on the base were a mass of brilliant yellows, reds, and a myriad of shades in between. The grass was still green. It was an unforgettable picture—especially with a cloudless blue sky in a late afternoon. The Marine Corps honor guard, in dress uniform, would be seen marching smartly across the parade ground in preparation for sounding retreat.

When a small cannon was fired, all personnel outdoors faced the flag and saluted as the bugle sounded. The flag, fluttering in the breeze, would be slowly lowered, coming to rest as the last sound of retreat echoed across the parade ground. The flag was carefully folded and, in the custody of those proud Marines, carried away. It would be returned the following morning and raised again in an equally impressive ceremony.

Our air group training at Quonset Point had been completed and we were ready to take one more step toward duty with the fleet. In mid- October the air group received orders to proceed to the west coast—NAS Alameda, California. Four days leave was arranged for those who lived near enough to Quonset Point to visit family and friends. The rest of us remained on duty.

"Soupy" Campbell was, by Academy definition, the "leader" of the squadron. As such, he always chose to be first when it came to any squadron activity. And, as his wing men, Jim McGee and I always shared that pleasure. Wherever or whenever, our section and division was number one. "Soupy's" comment would invariably be: "My division will take that flight."

And, when it came time for the squadron to fly to the west coast, "Soupy" was in the lead, followed by McGee and Bush and the remainder of our 36 planes. We had 48 crews (pilots/gunners) as well as ground personnel to man those airplanes and keep them flying. Those who did not have the privilege of flying to the coast got to ride the train.

We departed NAS Quonset Point on 31 October 1943. Because of uncertain weather to the west, we flew the southern route. Norfolk, Virginia was our first refueling stop and NAS Atlanta was our first overnight. The second night was at an Army Air Force base in Shreveport, LA. Foul weather delayed us for two days. Then, it was on to Midland, TX.

On arrival at Midland, it was found that one of our planes had developed a serious oil leak through a crack in a valve rocker box cover. It was necessary to take the rocker box cover over to the main airfield where it could be welded and machined. Bob Ricks was assigned the task of flying Harry Scholar, one of our ground crew Aviation Machinist mates over to the main base and have the repairs made. On return, Bob, in the true Navy tradition, wanted to impress the Air Force with a standard Navy approach. That is, coming downwind, parallel to the landing runway. Then, making a standard rate turn toward the runway, coming over the end of the runway still in a turn, leveling the wings, and landing with the tail wheel touching down just before the front wheels meet the paving.

The Air Force was impressed.   Bob had neglected to lower his wheels. Harry described the landing as very smooth.

On arriving in Tucson, we found that we had two crews/planes missing. This was our first loss of members since the squadron was formed. For an unexplained reason there had been a midair collision of the two planes which were supposed to have been in a widely spread formation. No one saw the collision and it wasn't until several days later that the wreckage and bodies were found in a remote region of west Texas.

NAS San Diego was our first overnight on the West Coast. The next day, we flew to NAS Alameda on San Francisco Bay. We found that the base was overtaxed and our squadron had been assigned to a brand new outlying auxiliary field in Santa Rosa—about 60 miles north of San Francisco. This was to be our home for the next six weeks. Allowable expenses for our cross country flight amounted to $7.00 per day if no government quarters were available, $3.00 per day if they were.

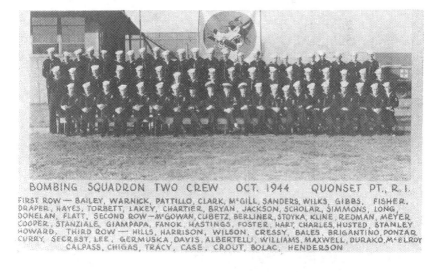

BOMBING SQUADRON TWO CREW   OCT. 1944   QUONSET PT., R. I.

FIRST ROW — BAILEY, WARNICK, PATTILLO, CLARK, M°GILL, SANDERS, WILKS, GIBBS, FISHER, DRAPER, HAYES, TORBETT, LAKEY, CHARTIER, BRYAN, JACKSON, SCHOLAR, SIMMONS, LONG, DONELAN, FLATT, SECOND ROW—M°GOWAN, CUBETZ, BERLINER, STOYKA, KLINE, REDMAN, MEYER, COOPER, STANZIALE, GIAMPAPA, FANOK, HASTINGS, FOSTER, HART, CHARLES, HUSTED, STANLEY, HOWARD, THIRD ROW — HILLS, HARRISON, WILSON, CRESSY, BALES, BRIGANTINO, PONZAR, CURRY, SECREST, LEE, GERMUSKA, DAVIS, ALBERTELLI, WILLIAMS, MAXWELL, DURAKO, M°ELROY, CALPASS, CHIGAS, TRACY, CASE, CROUT, BOLAC, HENDERSON

Figure 26. Bombing Squadron Two Crew October 1943.

Santa Rosa

Santa Rosa was a town of about 8000 population with the Naval Air Station southwest of town and an Army Air Force field on the north side. We were the first squadron to use the field, followed a few days later by our torpedo squadron. The fighters did not join us in Santa Rosa. They were pressed into service immediately. After being transported to Hawaii, they went aboard ship for action during the invasion of the Gilbert Islands. We would be rejoined in March, 1944, in Hilo, Hawaii.

Our training continued with gunnery and dive bombing exercises over the Pacific Ocean. Weather was typical for the north California coast in winter—heavy coastal fog at times in the morning, clearing inland during the day, resulting in beautiful flying weather.

It was during the Thanksgiving Day week that Margie Ann took a week off from the University of Idaho in Moscow, climbed aboard a train, and came to Santa Rosa to spend a few days with me before the-soon-to come departure. Her enlistment in the WAFs in May, 1943 had not been a successful venture and she had returned to her studies at the University of Idaho in the fall. She resided in the Santa Rosa Hotel, and I had my room at the base. It was an enjoyable but short visit. A few days later, she was back on the train, leaving the Oakland train station, bound for Portland, Oregon and then Spokane, Washington.

On 20 December, orders were received for the dive bombing and torpedo squadrons to report to NAS Alameda in preparation for "shipping out." The bombing squadron arrived at Alameda with 23 aircraft—visibility was below minimum—the red light on the tower indicated the field was closed. We landed anyway. There were no admonishments from the FAA or the Navy.

To The Pacific

On 22 December 1943, the USS Coral Sea sailed for Pearl Harbor, with a destroyer as escort in the lead. Aboard were Bombing Squadron - 2, Torpedo Squadron - 2, our planes, flight crews, and support personnel. The hangar and flight decks were filled with aircraft.

The USS Coral Sea was of a class of aircraft carriers built on a merchant hull by the Kaiser shipyards. They were identical in design and were being turned out at a rapid rate. They were used primarily as escort carriers to protect convoys in the Atlantic and for support of invasions in the Pacific theater. In addition, they were used to ferry replacement aircraft and naval personnel to the combat areas.

In tactical operations, they carried fighter aircraft and torpedo planes. The length of the deck was not adequate for the operation of dive bombers. The ships were approximately 430 feet in length with a flight deck 80 feet in width. The flight deck was about 60 feet, six stories, above the water line.

It was on such a ship we sailed under the Golden Gate Bridge that cool, grey December day. There was a strong wind out of the north, and it was not long before we encountered a quartering swell that diminished the authority of the USS Coral Sea to insignificance. Those swells had originated in the Gulf of Alaska and were the result of strong northwesterly gales.

**Figure 27. The USS Coral Sea CVE-57 underway in 1943.
Its name was later changed to the USS Anzio so a new large
Fleet Carrier could assume that very significant name.**

That small ship plowed into the massive swells, twisting and turning, rising, falling and complaining with each peak or valley with which it was confronted. The ship would climb one of the huge swells; the flight deck slanted to port, at the crest there would be a momentary pause with the bow nearly out of the water. The ship would come upright, the decks would rotate to starboard, the screw would come out of the water, there would be a momentary shudder, and then we plunged, as though on a surf board, toward a trough leading to the next swell.

There were expansion joints in the ship to accommodate the difference in movement of the hull, between the bow and the stern, when encountering foul weather. On the flight deck level, the movement of the joints was evident in sight and sound. The sounds were truly impressive with loud clangs and groans. We questioned the integrity of the ship and its ability to survive. It did survive.

Because of the unusual movement of the ship, many of the passengers and crew members were afflicted with motion sickness. Nearly everyone was seasick. It was a tough few days. Quarters were cramped and temperatures inside the ship were uncomfortably warm. There were eighteen of us in a compartment about ten feet by 20 feet. Bunks were intimately spaced in layers of three.

Three days after departure a traditional Christmas dinner was served—turkey, mashed potatoes, gravy, and dressing. Fresh milk was still to be had. By that time, the rough seas were diminishing, the temperatures were in a warming trend, and gradually the passage became enjoyable.

Diamond Head, on the island of Oahu, appeared the morning of 1 January 1944. When we sailed into Pearl Harbor later that morning, the impact of the Japanese attack two years before was still dramatically evident. There was the hulk of the USS Arizona and other wreckage. Battleships were still under repair. Activities at Pearl Harbor and on Ford Island were in a dynamic state 24 hours a day, seven days per week. The true importance of the 7 December 1941 attack really came into stark being. There was no question: there was a war to be won!

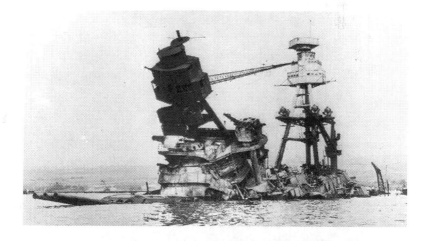

Figure 28. The burned-out, sunken wreck of Arizona (BB-39), photographed some days after the attack.

We didn't linger in Pearl Harbor. As soon as the planes were hoisted from the deck to Ford Island, they were fueled and prepared for flight. 4 January 1944—being in the "skippers" division, I enjoyed the privilege of flying to NAS Hilo, Hawaii, the big island, where we would be continuing our training prior to our next assignment.

The squadron flew south from Oahu, out over the channel past the low lying island of Molokai, then past Maui with its two large volcanic cones and the broad valley in between. From there it was down the east side of Hawaii, Mauna Kea and Mauna Loa to the west, steep black volcanic cliffs along the coast, and into the new NAS Hilo.

Those who didn't get to fly to Hilo had the privilege of sailing on a small inter-costal steamer through troubled waters— with the accompanying motion sickness and discomfort. There were stops at Molokai and Maui enroute, further delaying arrival in Hilo.

Hilo, Hawaii

The next two months brought periods of intensive training. Again, there were the squadron dive bombing activities using the armored PT boats as targets. The fighter squadron rejoined the air group after the invasion of the Gilberts, where they had offered support through air cover and strafing. There were the "group gropes" and, of great importance, the bombing squadron would be presented with replacement aircraft. Our beloved Douglas Dauntless dive bombers were to be replaced with the Curtiss SB2C Helldiver, known as "The Beast."

The stay on the island of Hawaii was an enjoyable one. There were days off when we visited the small town of Hilo. It was a community primarily of citizens of Japanese descent. Navy personnel did not demonstrate animosity toward the local citizens, even though many of them could only speak Japanese. However, Marines who had returned to Hawaii, on temporary assignment, after the difficult and bloody invasions in the Gilbert

Islands, frequently considered these people as little different from the enemy.

The Hilo business community consisted of one main street which ran parallel to the harbor. Many of the structures were of wood and had been constructed early in the century. The lower elevations of Hilo were subsequently inundated by a huge tidal wave shortly after the war, and a number of people were drowned.

One of the pleasures of Hilo was a visit to the local barber shop. It was family operated, with the Japanese father in charge and the daughters doing the hair cutting. After carefully trimming one's hair, they gently massaged the neck, applied lotion to the face and gave an additional tender touch to finish the task. It was worth the price of a haircut just for the extra attention.

There were visits to scenic sites—black sand beaches, the Kilauea crater, sugar cane fields and waterfalls in the state parks. Steak dinner in the dining room of the Hilo Hotel, with its manicured grounds and majestic palm trees along the shore of the Pacific Ocean was always a treat. The tropical weather was seductive. It would have been idyllic if the thought of future responsibilities had not lingered in the background.

Taming the "Beast"

In mid-February, we were told that we would be getting Bombing Squadron Eight's well worn SB2Cs (Helldivers) prior to our going aboard USS Hornet. The Navy had made the decision as early as 1938, when the SBD first went into production, they would need a replacement which would be faster, have a longer range, and carry a heavier bomb load. The SB2C was the aircraft chosen to be the replacement.

The difficulties and challenges involved with producing such an aircraft with the desired objectives is beyond the scope of this journal. Let it be said there were numerous problems.

During the testing of the SB2C, it became known as "The Large Tail Beast." That was subsequently shortened to "The Beast."

Figure 29. The Curtiss SB2C first flew in 1940 and required many modifications and a good pilot to make a worthy replacement of the SBD.

The Helldiver could carry a two thousand pound bomb in an internal bomb bay, exceeding the SBD's limited 1600 pound bomb load, carried externally under the belly of the aircraft. The loads of both planes could be varied with small bombs being carried on racks under the wings.

The SB2C Helldiver had a wing span of 50 feet and a length of 37 feet. Its wings folded for carrier operation. The gross weight was about 14,000 pounds. The engine of our SB2C-1Cs was a Wright R-2600-8 Cyclone with 1700 hp takeoff power. The armament consisted of two 20 mm cannons in the wings, firing forward and two flexible .30 caliber machine guns in the rear cockpit.

The three blade propeller was an unreliable electrically controlled, constant speed device, which invariably went into full low pitch at the most inconvenient moment. There were three different hydraulic systems—all prone to failure when least expected. Its range was listed as 1100 miles, but that must have been with gasoline tanks installed in the bomb bay.

The SBD was, in contrast, an aviator's airplane. It was stable and forgiving. In level flight, it could be trimmed to fly hands off for an almost indefinite period. In a dive-bombing attack, with flaps split, it seemed to hang in the air and could be flown as readily in the dive as when in normal flight. One could twist, turn, increase or decrease the angle of attack, and place the bomb directly on the target.

The Curtiss Helldiver (The Beast) was a challenge from the moment one took off until the plane was landed and back in the chocks. On the ground the engine tended to overheat because the large spinner around the propeller hub limited air flow over the cylinder heads. If the cylinder head temperatures were too high during takeoff, it was common to experience a partial loss of power due to detonation when at full throttle. That created anxieties.

The configuration of cockpit controls in the Beast was extremely poor. In order to retract the wheels, the pilot had to release his shoulder harness, lean forward, change hands on the stick, and actuate the wheel retraction lever which was on the forward, right side of the cockpit. In the meantime, there was no hand on the throttle. If the flaps were down (carrier takeoff), one was confronted with the further difficulty of gradually retracting them—all of this while flying at a low altitude and only slightly above stalling speed.

Ordinarily an airplane could be trimmed so it maintained a stable flight path. The SBD could be trimmed so it would fly almost perfectly "hands off." "Trimming" was accomplished by adjusting very small airfoils on the ailerons and elevator from the cockpit. In the event an SBD was trimmed slightly nose down, the nose would drop. The airplane would pick up speed, increasing lift, and eventually start to climb again. It would oscillate. With each oscillation the range of up or down would become less and eventually the airplane would be flying in a steady flight—slightly nose down.

Not so the SB2C Helldiver! The airplane was impossible to trim so it would fly "hands off." If a carefully trimmed Helldiver was slightly nose down, and left to fly on its own, the nose would drop—speed would increase and the nose would drop further. There was no recovery, no oscillation. If one did not take corrective action, the airplane would continue to increase the steepness of its flight path and eventually bury itself in the ground, or ocean.

If the SB2C was trimmed so it was flying nose up, the nose would continue to rise until the plane stalled, and went into a spin. Again, unless corrective action was taken, the plane would bury itself. The Beast had to be flown every minute. That instability was caused by having a shorter fuselage than an optimum design called for. The Navy wanted an aircraft with dimensions which allowed two planes to be raised or lowered at one time on the elevators, thus requiring the shorter fuselage. I never saw more than one SB2C on the elevators at one time during our tour.

When it came to dive bombing in the SB2C, it was essential that the proper angle of attack be established at the very beginning of the dive. Once into the attack, the Beast could not be maneuvered properly to correct for misjudgment or pilot error. In addition to these undesirable flight characteristics, the dive flaps were totally inadequate for the size and weight of the plane. It dove like its predecessor, the SBC—another streamlined safe.

And, so it was, in late February, 1944, with about three hours of flight time in the SB2C and two weeks before going aboard ship, we were taking field carrier landing practice. The moment was drawing near. On 3 March, the air group was transferred to NAS Barber's Point on the island of Oahu, west of Pearl Harbor. This would be the final training period before going aboard the USS Hornet (CV-12).

USS Hornet CV-12

USS Hornet (CV-12) was the eighth ship in the U.S. Navy to bear the name, and the second aircraft carrier. She replaced the USS Hornet (CV-8) which had been lost in the Battle of Santa Cruz on 26 October 1942. She was a ship of the Essex class, 29,000 tons displacement and a speed of over 32 knots. (One nautical mile per hour, one knot, is equal to 1.15 English miles per hour). Her overall length was 872 feet, her flight deck 110 feet wide. She had three elevators to transfer planes to and from the hangar deck: one forward, one aft, and one on the port side.

When her keel was laid, she was to be the USS Kearsarge. However, with the loss of USS Hornet (CV-8), it was decided to change the name of Kearsarge to Hornet to maintain that name in the fleet.

Figure 30. Hellcats get refueled and armed.

USS Hornet (CV-12) was commissioned on 29 November 1943 at the Norfolk Navy Yard, Portsmouth, Virginia, with a crew of 3000. After a short shakedown cruise, modifications followed to qualify the ship for combat. With an urgency to rush the ship into service in the Pacific Fleet, she sailed in February for Pearl Harbor.

Hornet was equipped with four radar-directed twin turret, five inch anti-aircraft batteries—all located on the flight deck—two forward and two aft of the island. In addition, there were four single five inch guns. Numerous radar-directed 40 mm quads (four guns to a battery) were located in gun tubs on both sides of the ship just below the flight deck. There was also a set of 40 mm quads on the fantail at hangar deck level, one set of quads at the bow, and many batteries of single 20 mm anti-aircraft guns on the port and starboard sides which were manually operated. It was a formidable array of weapons and one which would prove to be an able defense.

Figure 31. The Quad 40 mm guns of the Hornet on 16 February 1945 as TF-58 planes were raiding Tokyo. Note expended shells and ready-service ammo stored on the right.

Hornet arrived in Pearl Harbor on 4 March 1944, just one day after we arrived at NAS Barber's Point. During a ten day delay, the ship was further outfitted for combat duty. Air Group 2 was finalizing field carrier landing practice flights and preparing for the actual carrier qualifications.

As part of planning for departure, I went to the Officer's Club and bought two bottles of Canadian Club whiskey to take along. The objective was to have something of value to trade with the troops on the islands where we might be anchoring. Both bottles traveled well over a hundred thousand miles across the Pacific Ocean and were never opened. They eventually were carried back to the U.S. and given to Romey Taylor when I was on leave in October 1944.

On 8 March, we checked out on Hornet with four carrier landings each. The SB2C again demonstrated the instability so prevalent in its flight characteristics. One absolutely had to be flying this Beast every moment! It was a far cry from that stable SBD. Then, back to the beach for a few more days and the procurement of brand new SB2C-1Cs requisitioned from Bombing Squadron 15. We were ready to go.

March 13 was another day of training. This time, twenty four of us, pilots and gunners, flew our airplanes fifty miles out to the southwest of Oahu where we met Hornet, and with the fighter and torpedo squadrons, landed aboard. The ship would return to Pearl the next day when the remainder of the squadron would come aboard. While enroute to port, those of us who were on the ship would conduct an early morning "group grope."

The early morning flight on the 14th was less than stellar. The pre-dawn launch was truly disorganized! "Soupy", the squadron skipper failed to turn on his running lights, and it was impossible to find him. The fighters also had a difficult time— they were joining up on the bombers and we were joining up on the fighters. Chaos! It wasn't until two hours later (daylight) that we all finally got together and completed the training exercise. We did manage to make two successful dive bombing runs on a towed sled behind Hornet, using 100 pound water filled bombs. We hoped that day's confusion wasn't a sign of things to come.

It was back to Pearl for the night. Remaining members of the air group came aboard, and we sailed the morning of 15 March 1944 in a task group with two Independence class carriers, two heavy cruisers, and nine destroyers which acted as a screen for the heavier ships. A comparable force was directly behind us. The weather was comfortably warm, the seas calm. Majuro, an atoll anchorage in the southern Marshalls, was our destination.

There were two familiarization flights while we were enroute, to give us and the ship's crew additional training. Carrier operations were demanding for both the air and deck crews, and the additional experience would be helpful in the operations to come.

The following events would become standard as we proceeded through our training flights and into combat. Prior to takeoff, air crews were briefed by the intelligence officer in their ready rooms concerning the upcoming flight. The ready room was the center of activity for the squadron members. We were there most of the day, and frequently into the night—whether we were preparing for a flight, or just marking time. There were only a few air conditioned spaces on the ship, and the ready room was one of them.

The ready room was our battle station at General Quarters. Every morning, one hour before dawn, it was standard procedure for the ship to go to General Quarters. It was a period when the fleet was particularly vulnerable to submarine attack. The ship would then be in a state of readiness if such an attack did occur. We would all be present, in the soft leather chairs, trying to get a little more sleep.

**Figure 32. The Ready Room where missions were briefed
and pilots could occasionally relax.**

It was a comfortable compartment, with the rows of reclining chairs. The chairs had school room type desks attached that folded down to one side. The desk's primary use was for navigation calculations prior to flight operations. However, at other times they were also used for letter writing and reading; perhaps a game of solitaire. A few hammocks, strung in the overhead, allowed accommodations for one to sleep horizontally—if you got there early enough. A large blackboard and teletype machine with screen were at the front, providing pertinent information which originated from a central source in the ship.

Across the passageway was a small pantry, where an assigned messmate prepared sandwiches and beverages for those pilots who were on flights which conflicted with normal dining hours. Roland E. Williams was our man. He was a young short stocky Black youth in his late teens with a round face and very close cropped hair. His primary goal was to finish the war and go to hair dressers school. He enjoyed describing the profession and expounding on the number of different bones in one's head—how the structure of the head required special attention to the accompanying hair.

Once the flight schedule had been determined and flight crews were standing by, essential information was provided. The ship's position and course were defined, the target established, weather information (including temperatures, wind direction and velocity) were provided. Necessary information was transferred to the plotting boards and navigation parameters were established. The latest information concerning radio aides to navigation (ZB) was recorded and the flight crews were ready to go. Our radio aid to navigation consisted of a rotating antennae which sent a different Morse code signal about every 15 degrees from the carrier. When receiving such a signal, the pilot could fly a 180 degree reciprocal heading to locate the ship. This aid to navigation was received on ultra high frequency and only as "a line of sight." At 100 miles from the carrier, the plane had to be at an altitude of at least 10,000 feet of altitude. A final comment on the teletype revealed the water temperature— always an item of interest. There were occasions when one ended up in the water, and you knew in advance, what the comfort level would be. The water temperatures were usually in the mid-80's.

At the announcement, "Pilots, man your planes," the air crews moved rapidly from the ready rooms to the flight deck. On deck, the planes were positioned to maximize space. Propellers were only inches behind the plane in front. Folded wings were side by side, with only a few inches between. Tie-down lines had been removed but wheels were still firmly secured in their chocks.

The flight crews would make their way under the noses of the parked planes, around the wheels, up on the wings and then the final step into the cockpits. The deck crews in their color coded helmets and shirts were standing by ready for the start of engines, removal of chocks, and movement of the planes forward into takeoff position.

Yellow Shirts: Flight Deck Officers and Plane Directors. The only people on the flight deck authorized to move aircraft, or give hand signals to move.

Green Shirts: Catapult and Arresting Gear people. Operate, and maintain the Catapults and Arresting Gear. Squadron Aircraft Maintenance people also were green.

Red Shirts: Aviation ordnance crews. Load and "arm" those weapons on the aircraft. Sometimes referred to as "BB Stackers", or "Ordies".

Checker shirts: Squadron maintenance Quality Control people. Responsible for final overall checks of a/c readiness before launch.

Blue Shirts: Flight deck crew, work under direction of a Yellow Shirt as part of a crew. Plane pushers/handlers; chock planes, push planes, scrub decks—do all the tough jobs.

Brown Shirts: Squadron personnel—Plane Captains. (No ship's company wear brown shirts.)

Purple shirts: Aviation fuels people. Referred to as "Grapes". Gas aircraft. Operate & maintain carrier avgas/jet fuel/ av lube oil systems.

White shirts: Mail and people handlers for carrier on board delivery (COD).

There were the preliminary procedures after entering the cockpit, with the plane captain, in his brown T-shirt and helmet, helping the pilot. The pilot and gunner connected the parachute harnesses to the chutes, which were already in the seat of the airplane. Make sure all fastenings were secure—then unfasten the chest and leg straps so that on takeoff one would not be encumbered if a water landing ensued. The chute was reattached after gaining altitude.

We would initially connect oxygen tubing and masks, radio cords to the earphones, and shoulder and lap safety belts. Then, go through the preliminary check off list. Patience. Wait. The ship was sailing downwind and there was little wind over the deck. Silence. Soon, from the bridge, the word came over the PA system, "Pilots, Start Engines." In the crowded confines of the flight deck, the plane captain checked to insure the propeller area was clear and then gave a "thumbs up."

Both magnetos were turned to the "on" position—the engine was primed with the electric fuel pump, throttle set, mixture rich, propeller positioned in full low pitch—starter switch on—the propeller turned slowly—cough—pause—rumble—there was a momentary surge as the engine came to life and black smoke briefly poured from the exhaust. Then there was the steady rumble of the Curtiss Wright's double-bank 18 cylinder radial engine. All instruments were checked to insure the system was operating properly. Go through the check off list again. Stand by.

Figure 33. The flight deck comes alive with the order "Pilots start your engines."

The ship, which had been on a specific course, or on a zigzag pattern, came into the wind. With the wind down the deck, the Fox flag (Foxtrot in the 1990's), white, with a red square rotated 45 degrees from its background, was flying "at the dip," two thirds of the way up the halyard. That was an indication that the ship was preparing for flight operations. With the wind down the deck, the Fox flag was "two blocked," run to the top of the halyard. There was no further delay. The ship did not want to be in the vulnerable position of staying on a straight course any longer than absolutely necessary. Launch planes!

Fighters took off first to establish air cover. Wings on the fighters (Hellcats/F6Fs) were not actuated hydraulically. They had been manually folded into position alongside the fuselage. When readied for takeoff, the wings were released manually by the deck crews. With the help of gravity, the wings were swung down through an arc and then, with physical force by the deck crew, into flight position where they were locked.

Figure 34. The hellcats launched first, their wings had to be manually unfolded.

Because of their power, fighters needed less deck for takeoff than the following planes. With the Hellcat, the pilot sat close to the engine and the exhaust stacks were nearly in his face. There was a flat, popping sound from the exhaust as the plane rapidly picked up speed. The Hellcats leapt from the bow, and at the same moment, the pilot began retracting the landing gear, by simply moving a lever in the dashboard to the "up" position. The gear rotated 90 degrees, and the wheels were at right angles to their normal position as they were swept back and up into the wings in the fashion of a raptor becoming airborne. A plane was launched every 30 seconds.

The Turkeys (torpedo planes) were next, needing little deck space to become airborne. The Turkeys were ungainly machines. They perched on long spindly legs with wheels at the bottom. The fuselage was large and bulbous, to accommodate bombs, or a 20 foot torpedo. The pilot was sitting in a crow's-nest, looking out over wide, long wings which had just been unfolded hydraulically from alongside the fuselage. One crew member was in an electrically operated gun turret behind the pilot, and another gunner was in the tunnel behind the bomb bay.

Figure 35. Launching the Grumman TBF Avengers.

When the launching officer, *Fly One*, in his yellow T-shirt and helmet, sent a Turkey on its way, it moved slowly. Weight came slowly off the landing gear struts; the struts extended, wheels bounced, but came off the deck long before the plane reached the bow. The wheels actually stopped turning before the plane passed over the bow and the gear was retracted.

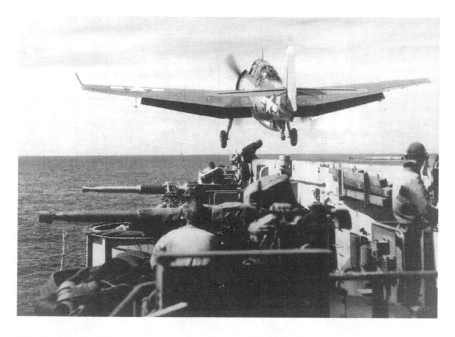

Figure 36. The close proximity of the deck crew is obvious in this launch of a TBF

Again, the awkwardness of the Turkey was emphasized as the wheels on their long spindly legs raised outward, and finally found their way into the lower side of the wings. In spite of the ugly appearance of the Avenger, it was one of the best flying airplanes in the fleet.

Last were the bombers, needing every available foot of deck. The plane was taxied out of position very carefully, following the directions by the deck traffic crew, toward the takeoff spot. Only inches separated the planes in their parked positions.

When clear, the deck crew gave arm signals to unfold the wings, which had been folded overhead. They were hydraulically actuated, moving into flight position. With the wings extended, a locking mechanism was actuated by the pilot in the cockpit, and warning flags in the wings were retracted, indicating the plane was ready for flight. The deck crew visually inspected the locking mechanism to insure the wings were positively in the locked position. More hand signals—flaps down for takeoff. Then it is to the takeoff position and brakes were set.

Figure 37. Below the flight deck is the hanger deck.

As the plane ahead was rolling down the flight deck, toward the bow, *Fly One* instructed the pilot to turn up the engine to near takeoff power by waving one finger in a tight circle. After a quick check of the instrument panel and finding everything acceptable, the pilot gave an affirmative nod.

Fly One immediately responded with a two finger turn up—go to maximum takeoff power! The engine was at full throttle and the plane vibrating as it was restrained by the brakes. The pilot did one more check—OK. There was a second affirmative nod. *Fly One* checked one more time to insure the forward deck was not fouled. All clear! At that moment, giving the takeoff signal, his right hand moved swiftly toward the bow, small flag standing out in the brisk wind. He was in the familiar position frequently seen of WW-2 carrier operations, crouched low, to avoid the wing as it passed over his head. Go!

Brakes were released and the plane slowly picked up speed. There was already about 30 knots of wind over the deck. Without a bomb load, the tail came up readily. With a bomb load, it was a different story. As the plane approached the bow, it was nearly ready to fly. The tail had been brought to a three point position and the plane became airborne, struggling over the bow.

A very careful right hand turn was made to clear the deck of prop wash, then a gentle turn to the left to conform to the course of the ship. Get the gear up! At one of the most critical moments in the flight, the pilot went through the life threatening procedure of releasing the shoulder harness, changing hands on the stick, throttle left to its own devises, head down in the cockpit -grab that landing gear handle, which was far forward on the right side of the cockpit, and GET THE GEAR UP! Then secure the shoulder harness again! Gradually the flaps were retracted and flying speed was slowly increased.

Next came the task of trimming the aircraft for flight. Cowl flaps were closed by use of the hand crank. Full rich mixture (for takeoff) was reduced to normal cruising position; the desired manifold pressure and propeller speed (pitch) were established. Keep your eye on the plane ahead and on that of the division leader if possible.

There were occasions when the airplane did not fly when it passed over the bow. Splash! Twenty nine thousand tons of aircraft carrier were bearing down on the plane and crew at speeds up to 25 knots. Alarms were instantly sounded! There was no time to spare! The ship's helmsman immediately applied full left rudder, moving the bow to port and swinging the stern of the ship to starboard. Within moments, he followed with full right rudder, moving the bow to starboard and swinging the stern to port. That took the ship on a path which barely curved around the sinking plane and the crew. Smoke pots were thrown overboard as the ship sailed past the scene of the accident, only a few feet away from the side of the ship.

The guard destroyer, standing by to the rear of the carrier, "came to," launched a motor whale boat and attempted to recover the plane's crew. Even if they had survived the crash, it could be difficult to find them in choppy waters. That operation was not always successful. A water landing during pre-dawn operations made recovery of the crew even more difficult. During our tour of duty, three crews were lost to launching accidents —all occurred during daylight operations.

Normal operations called for the division leader to fly out ahead of the ship on the same course. After five minutes, he would make a left hand 180 degree turn. This would allow each of the following planes in the division the opportunity of turning inside of him and joining up by the time the flight had come abeam the carrier. The flight then climbed to altitude and circled above the carrier until all members had joined the formation.

In theory, the plan worked well. In actuality, it was a team effort that required every member of the flight to perform at a high level of proficiency. One had to be disciplined in every aspect of the launch and the follow through.

When the air group's three squadrons were all in the same sky, the bombers led the way to the target. Usually twelve dive bombers were airborne, as two divisions of six planes each. The second division flew formation on the group leader. Eight torpedo planes were close by in two formations of four each. The fighters, sixteen in number, were above, flying cover in their scissor type crossovers in groups of four.

The other Essex class carrier in the task group was also launching a similar effort. In addition, two Independence class carriers (CVLs) were providing fighter and torpedo bomber support to the overall operation. CVLs were medium sized carriers built on a cruiser hull. They did not carry dive bombers.

Once all aircraft were airborne, the entire flight departed the task group for the assigned target. The senior naval aviator aloft assumed responsibility for directing the attack.

On return to the ship, the air group circled the ship with the fighters descending first to the lowest altitude. Another group of fighters flew combat air patrol at high altitude above the task group. They were under the control of the Combat Information Center (CIC) and would be radar directed to intercept any enemy aircraft that might be in the area.

Figure 38. The Hornet's Combat Information Center (CIC) was a darkened room.

The fighters were in the landing circle ready to come aboard as soon as the ship came into the wind. With experience, the first plane was "in the groove" ready for the cut the moment the ship had established the proper wind down the deck.

Fighters came aboard at a speed noticeably faster than the Turkeys and the Beasts. The pilot's cockpits were up forward, close behind the engines of the Hellcats and visibility was excellent. They could easily see the Landing Signal Officer (LSO) during the entire approach and respond to every signal.

They would come out of their turn over the fantail, get a cut, and then impressively, slam down on the deck. Sometimes there would be blown tires and the plane would limp forward on floppy tires.

In any event, the next few moments passed rapidly. Flight deck crews emerged from the catwalks at a run! The tail hook was released from the arresting cable, three flight deck crewmen from each side grasped the wings, which had been unlocked, and swung them into the folded position alongside the fuselage. At the same time, the pilot began taxiing the plane forward to get ahead of the barriers.

Figure 39. The Landing Signal Officer—LSO, also known as "Paddles" or "The Maestro." The landing plane was low in this approach.

Next came the torpedo planes in their slow, stable, lumbering approach. They appeared to be suspended in flight. Visibility was excellent, as the pilot was perched high on the forward end of that bulbous fuselage. As they came over the fantail, in slow motion, they received a cut, hovered for a few moments, and then settled slowly to the deck, being easily brought to a halt by the arresting gear. Torpedo planes could be, and were on occasion, brought aboard without benefit of tail hook without crashing into the barriers.

Then it was the bombers turn. The two divisions had been circling the carrier as a flight. In preparation for landing, they would divide the two divisions into individual flights. The first division proceeded upwind on the starboard side of the ship with the two sections maneuvered into right echelons. The second division waited its turn.

It was at this point that the flight leader gave the signal for landing gear and tail hooks to come down. Careful visual observation by fellow pilots would confirm that landing gear was down and locked and that the tail hook was extended—ready for landing.

The leader broke off in a left hand turn as soon as the landing circle permitted entry. Succeeding planes followed at thirty second intervals which subsequently resulted in one minute spacing on the downwind leg. A well executed operation could land planes at the rate of one per minute.

Bringing the Beast aboard a carrier was always a challenge. We would make the left hand turn into the landing circle, establishing the appropriate interval when we turned to the downwind leg. The landing gear, flaps, and tail hook—were down. Fuel supply on reserve, mixture—full rich, propeller—full low pitch, cowl flaps open, parachute harness unfastened, shoulder and lap safety belts locked. Complete the check off list. Establish an altitude of about 100 feet and a speed of about 80 knots.

Cockpit canopies were in the locked open position. One did not want to end up in the water with a canopy that had slammed shut on impact. Nor did one want to come to a rapid halt in the arresting gear and have the canopy propelled to the closed position.

**Figure 40. SB2C-3 Helldiver pilots returning to the Hornet
following strikes on Japanese shipping in the China Sea,
Circa mid-January 1945. (Photo by Lt Cmdr Charles Kerlee,
USNR)**

When abeam the fantail, with the ship just off the left
wing tip, we started a standard rate turn toward the ship.
Constant speed and altitude were maintained while remaining in
a continuous turn. The Landing Signal Officer (LSO) was kept
in sight at all times, even as the plane came over the fantail. Of
course, it wasn't quite that simple. It was difficult to stay within
the narrow limits of speed, altitude, and turn required for the
operation.

The Beast was notorious for its poor handling qualities.
At slow speeds, full power, flaps and landing gear down, it
lacked stability. In a nose-high attitude, visibility was poor.
Increased torque required the use of excessive top rudder, and
aileron response to the stick was almost non-existent. It was
heavy on the controls. One could rotate the stick in the cockpit
with little effect on control of the aircraft.

Once we achieved the hallowed position over the fantail, rolled our wings level and received a cut, there was no place to go but down. The Beast was ready to collapse. It sank like a rock. Crash! Bang! Jerk! The flight deck crew was out of the catwalks, the tail hook released from the arresting cable, and retracted into the rear of the fuselage. Wings were folding—taxi forward —expedite! There was another plane in the landing pattern, only moments behind.

Figure 41. Training accidents during ship and air group shakedown and workup were not infrequent. This Helldiver from VB-15 (15-B-25) had its tail chewed off by another SB2C.

It was a hazardous operation bringing a Helldiver aboard an aircraft carrier. We needed all of the help we could get and that was why we were pleased to have the assistance of our landing signal officer.

The landing signal officer could be compared to a symphony orchestra conductor. His "baton" consisted of two international orange cloth paddles. Each conductor had his own style and theater of performance. The LSO's podium was a six foot square platform on the after end of the flight deck on the port side. Instead of a symphony hall, his theater was the vast expanse of ocean being viewed from a flight deck six stories above the waves.

A six foot square canvas screen behind the LSO shielded him from the wind. The screen could be lowered rapidly in the event an airplane came dangerously near. A "talker," behind the LSO, kept him constantly informed of conditions on the flight deck. Both the LSO and the "talker" could leap over the side into a safety net several feet below in the event of an emergency.

The LSO had a responsible, exciting, and dangerous task. He was in the intimate proximity of fast moving aircraft as they came aboard, landing only a few feet away from his podium. An error on the part of the pilot or misjudgment by the LSO could result in loss of life and serious damage to the ship.

One never saw the signal officer standing woodenly, with paddles being moved in a deliberate manner. Instead, he would, unconsciously, assume the responsibilities of the maestro, and at the same time, perform as a ballet dancer. There would be a subtle fluid movement from side to side on his platform, with paddles in continuous flowing motion.

The incoming plane sometimes made a perfect approach. Frequently though it was too fast, slow, high, low, lacking flaps, the gear not down, angling for the deck—all of these deficiencies would be conveyed to the pilot through a system of semaphore signals. The LSO might even leave his platform, and move a few feet toward the center of the flight deck, to force the pilot into the desired groove. With a cut or a wave off, he finished with a pirouette. In a moment, a new scene would be choreographed.

Eight arresting cables, each about one and one-half inches in diameter stretched across the ship at intervals of about

40 feet. These were elevated mechanically six or eight inches above the deck, allowing the plane's hook to easily engage the wire. The cables passed through a system of pulleys leading below deck to a compartment containing a large hydraulic shock absorber and a pressure tank.

As the cable was pulled forward by the landing aircraft, the hydraulic plunger was actuated, forcing fluid into the high pressure tank which contained an air cap. Air pressure in the tank determined the length of cable that could be withdrawn when a plane landed. The higher the pressure, the less cable could be withdrawn. That resulted in a shorter landing distance, but created greater stress on the landing aircraft and the arresting gear.

Figure 42. This Hellcat went off the port side into the catwalk. A member of the deck crew is risking his life to help the pilot.

The usual procedure was to start with a relatively low pressure in the system actuated by the first cable. Pressure was incrementally increased in succeeding systems through the eighth cable. At that point, maximum pressure was established and a minimum of cable was drawn out, if engaged.

Flight deck operations presented many hazards. Turning propellers and landing aircraft in a very limited space was extremely dangerous. Accordingly, flight deck crews in the landing area always positioned themselves in the catwalks near an access to a lower deck in the event of an emergency. They did not leave the catwalks until conditions permitted safe access to the flight deck.

On occasions, an arresting cable would break when it was engaged. It was like a giant rubber band, snapping violently across the deck, over the catwalk, and down the side of the ship. At other times the landing aircraft would not be in the center of the deck, and after engaging the wire, would end up in the catwalk with the propeller still turning. On such occasions, caution was rewarded.

Figure 43. This SB2C failed to catch the wire on landing and hit the first barrier nosing into the deck.

In the event a tail hook broke off, or a plane came aboard too fast and did not catch a wire, there were always the barriers.

There were six of them, actuated in a similar manner to the arresting cables but with the capability of drawing out much less wire. They were about four feet above the deck and engagement with a barrier invariably resulted in the airplane tipping up on its nose, with a damaged propeller, or worse. Barriers could be raised and lowered as required when planes were taxiing from the landing area to the forward flight deck.

If an aircraft was taxiing through the barriers, it was standard procedure that the next airplane would not be allowed to land unless the three aft barriers were in the upright position. Ordinarily a plane would be brought aboard when the forward three barriers were in the up position and the three aft barriers were down. As the plane taxied forward, the sixth barrier would come up and the third barrier would come down. Next, the fifth barrier came up and barrier two came down. Last, the fourth barrier came up and barrier one came down.

When the plane was forward of the number one barrier, the first three barriers were once again brought to the upright position and the last three were down. By that time another plane was landing and the procedure was repeated.

The LSO was kept informed of deck conditions by his "talker" who was on the platform with him. With a sound powered telephone system, he was able to communicate with an observer up forward. If the barriers were in the proper configuration, planes could be landed. If more than three barriers were down, the landing aircraft would be waved off even though the approach had been acceptable.

Life Aboard Ship

Hornet was a magnificent ship to behold as it steamed regally through those warm Pacific waters. From the air, its course could be clearly defined as it cut through the ocean, leaving a broad churning wake to the stern. From the surface, its sides were a camouflage of intricate abstract designs—lines and colors ranged from dark grey to off-white. They were misleading, and the vessel's course was usually ill-defined. This ship would be our home for the next six months.

It was a new experience living aboard ship. Three officers were assigned to our stateroom. One porthole, with glass painted black, could be opened for ventilation when lights were extinguished, but it had to be closed during blackout conditions. Decks and furniture were of steel. Nothing was flammable except bedding, door curtains, and chair cushions.

My roommates were John Houston and Bos Bosworth. Both, along with their gunners, were subsequently lost to enemy action and an operational accident. John was shot down over Peleliu in the Palaus on 30 March on our first day of combat. Bos was lost three weeks later during a takeoff crash.

Figure 44. The Hornet's port-side camouflage pattern is clearly discernable.

Our eight foot by twelve foot room provided warm comfort. At one end were double bunks and at the other, against the sloping side of the ship, was the third bunk. Mine was the lower of the double bunks and particularly desirable since it had an electric fan directly above it. We each had a desk/bureau combination that provided drawer space for clothes and a fold down desk for letter writing. There were open spaces with clothes racks for uniforms. Each room had a telephone.

Central wash basins, shower, and toilet facilities were down the passageway. Sanitary facilities were flushed with salt water and effluent was discarded overboard. Wash basins and showers were provided with distilled water prepared in evaporators aboard ship. That effluent too was discarded overboard. Fresh water was always in short supply and demanded limited use. Its conservation was absolutely essential. Although the three single plate evaporators could produce up to 88,000 gallons of distilled water per day, most of it was required for the steam turbines driving the four mammoth propellers.

Showers consisted of wetting one's body with a very brief spray of water, soaping quickly, and rinsing briefly. Water for a shower probably didn't exceed two or three gallons.

Laundry allowed a change of underwear, socks, shirts, and trousers each day. Black messmates made up the rooms daily and changed sheets weekly. Personal laundry was also collected and washed weekly. The laundry used salt water for the initial wash and distilled water for the final rinse. Khaki shirts and trousers came back neatly ironed and stiffly starched.

We dined like the officers and gentlemen we were. The wardroom provided tables which were fixed to the deck. There were table cloths, sterling silver napkin rings, and cloth napkins which were changed twice per week. Lunch and dinner were served by Filipino or black waiters. Breakfast was cafeteria style with a variety of items on the menu.

Breakfast was my favorite meal: one could have eggs prepared to order, bacon and hotcakes. Ummmm. Really good. The menu for lunch and dinner was the same for officers and enlisted men. The only difference was where the food was prepared and the manner in which it was served.

The enlisted men were served cafeteria style and officers were served in the wardroom by messmates. Quality of the food was good to excellent. It was only after we had been underway for an extended period of time without a resupply of fresh meat and vegetables that the menus became tedious. At that point, all of the food came out of cans.

When engaged in combat, the wardroom could not accommodate the flight crews every hour of the day. It was then that we relied on the availability of sandwiches from our pantry and the good graces of our short, stocky, round faced Black messmate, with the close cropped hair, Roland E. Williams, Proprietor. He could always come up with some sustenance.

On one occasion, after a particularly stressful flight, I asked Roland to prepare a sandwich for me. After it was prepared, he handed me the plate and said, "Mr. Bush, your hands are trembling." I replied, "Roland, if you had been where I was, your hands would be trembling too."

Information of general concern to the ship's company was passed over the PA system by the quartermaster on duty. There were numerous standard type messages, each preceded by the shrill sound (call) of the boatswain's pipe. There was a special call for each type of message.

Periodically during the day one would hear the call, and then the command, "Sweepers, man your brooms, clean sweep down, fore and aft. Empty all trash cans." There was chow call, with a bugle to make it official. Because of the large number of personnel on the ship and the variable schedules required during battle operations, various divisions would be fed at different times to accommodate the launching and recovery of aircraft. Those schedules would be announced over the PA system.

An unforgettable announcement—the boatswain's pipe calling all hands. Next, "Now hear this, the man with the keys to the garbage grinder, lay down and open same— uhhhhmeediuuly." The boatswains were unable to pronounce the word "immediately." We assumed they did find the man with the keys to the garbage grinder since there were no follow up announcements.

There was one call and announcement to which everyone paid attention. Over the PA system, the boatswain's pipe sounded the call—all hands! Next came the announcement, "Now hear this, GENERAL QUARTERS! ALL HANDS, MAN YOUR BATTLE STATIONS!" That was followed by the loud continuous clanging of the bell reserved for the announcement of general quarters. Adrenaline was flowing!

Every man on the ship reported to his battle station on the double. Within minutes, all water tight doors and compartments were secured. Blowers were turned off throughout the ship to avoid the movement of flammable vapors in case of attack and spillage of bunker fuel or gasoline. Temperatures increased to uncomfortable levels. If one did not get to his battle station before the securing of water tight doors, he was confronted with opening and closing behind him as many doors as necessary to get to his station.

It was standard procedure that the ship would go to general quarters every morning an hour before daylight. It was a period of the day when the fleet was particularly vulnerable to submarine attack. When at general quarters, the ship would be prepared for a submarine attack. Everyone knew that. Every evening, an announcement would be made throughout the ship that general quarters would be sounded at a prescribed time the next morning.

The next morning, fifteen minutes prior to the actual sounding of general quarters there would be the boatswain's call of "all hands" and an announcement, "Now hear this, general quarters will be sounded in fifteen minutes." Fifteen minutes later, it was the real thing.

There were other calls on the boatswain's pipe and the bugle: Flight quarters, special scheduling of meals, first call for inspection, final call. When arriving in port the anchor party had their own call and an announcement informing them to standby. When the anchor was dropped there was a single blast of the bugle and an announcement of the time. Of course, there was a bugle call for the raising of the anchor.

Each evening, alternately, the Protestant and Catholic chaplains would recite the 23rd psalm over the PA system. I was always impressed with verse four: "Yea, though I walk through the valley of the shadow of death, I will fear no evil, for thou art with me. Thy rod and thy staff will comfort me" Taps followed the reading. It was a period of silence throughout the ship, a moment for meditation.

Anti-Submarine Patrol

During our voyage from Pearl Harbor to Majuro, we were conducting anti-submarine patrol. My turn came the day we were to arrive at Majuro. It was the first flight of the day and four of us were assigned to a pre-dawn catapult launch, each of us carrying two 500 pound depth bombs. Launching a few planes for anti-submarine patrol did not warrant turning the entire task group into the wind to launch planes. So, the anti-submarine patrols were launched from the catapult on whatever the course of the fleet. It was a new and exciting experience.

Carrying depth bombs was different than carrying a load of conventional high explosive bombs. There was the possibility that depth bombs might explode if a plane went in the water and sank to a depth of several hundred feet. In the event the crew had survived, they were still vulnerable to the explosion of those bombs. There wasn't anything a crew could do but hope they wouldn't become armed and explode. As a precaution, however, the crews were advised to float on their backs, minimizing the pressure to which the body would be subjected to at the time of explosion.

Leaving the ready room for the flight deck in the dark of night was impressive in itself. The ship was blacked out, and one had to make his way carefully through the maze of planes to the assigned aircraft, which seemed to assume monster proportions. Once in the cockpit, with the help of shielded lights, we made ready to for takeoff.

Under the direction of the flight deck crew, engines were started and we taxied out of the parked position. Wings were unfolded, flaps lowered to takeoff position, check off list completed, and then one at a time, planes were very carefully positioned on the catapult.

The catapult was an integral part of the flight deck. It was about 80 feet long with a slot down the center of the metal face plate through which a heavy steel hook moved. It was actuated by an extremely high pressure hydraulic system.

A braided steel cable harness was secured to the catapult hook by catapult crew members in their green t-shirts. Each end of the harness was attached to heavy hooks under the wings of the aircraft, adjacent to the landing gear. The harness remained secured to the catapult hook as the plane was being launched. The ends of the harness were released from the aircraft when it reached the end of the catapult.

Figure 45. A Grumman TBF is prepared for a catapult launch.

Once on the catapult, the system was brought up to pressure, the pilot completed his check off list and the flight deck crew made ready for launch. The pilot's head was pressed firmly back against a padded head rest. The left hand was on the throttle, with small finger wrapped around a hook designed for the occasion, to prevent the throttle hand from backing off during launch. The right hand held the stick loosely, with the elbow firmly planted in his gut. That was to prevent erratic movement of the controls at a crucial moment.

The preliminary engine turn up was completed, followed by the maximum power two finger turn up. An affirmative nod was given, the catapult officer gave the launch command, and we were on our way.

Wow! From a standing start, to 85 knots in a distance of 80 feet was impressive! There was no way that one could draw away from the back of the seat until we were off the deck, hurtling into the blackness of those tropical skies.

The total anti-submarine search area included an arc of about 200 degrees around the forward part of the task group. We each had a designated triangle which we flew—thirty miles out at an altitude of about 2000 feet, then a cross leg, and back to the fleet. The procedure would be repeated throughout the four hour flight—all of the time we were carefully looking for periscopes or signs of a submarine.

Submarine patrols were shared between the four carriers in the task group. On Hornet, the bombing and torpedo squadrons alternated the duty. During the six months we were flying patrols, we never saw any submarines.

On the morning of 20 March, the low lying islets of Majuro Atoll came into view. Its elevation was only a few feet above sea level, but the majestic palm trees, leaning over the lagoon, presented a beautiful idyllic scene. No Japanese garrison had been established there and no resistance had been encountered when our forces took over.

There was only one navigable entrance to the 90 square mile lagoon that defined the atoll of Majuro. We entered that pass, only a few hundred yards wide, into the lagoon, at an impressive speed of about 15 knots. Ships did not linger when in the vulnerable position presented on entering or leaving the lagoon, even though there were numerous destroyers and aircraft on anti-submarine patrol at the harbor entrance.

With our arrival, practically the entire Pacific fleet was anchored in Majuro lagoon. Three of the four carrier groups were there with an average of 16 destroyers for each screen. There were battleships, cruisers, tankers, supply ships and a hospital ship with its huge red cross on the side. The fleet stretched for miles. This was the assembly point for the fleet which would be supporting invasions soon to be taking place on the north coast of New Guinea and the enemy held Carolines.

Figure 46. A deck full of SB2C and Hellcats respond to the command "Start your engines."

I had a surprise visitor the day we dropped anchor in Majuro atoll. Jack Bohning, a fellow cadet at primary base, whose Pensacola training experiences paralleled mine, came on board looking for old friends. There we were, thousands of miles from the U.S., on a small atoll that none of us had ever heard of only a few months before.

On completion of his training, Jack had joined the Marine Corps and eventually ended up in an SBD dive bombing squadron, stationed on Majuro. It was a real pleasure seeing him again. We would meet again later on the atoll of Kwajalein— along with all but one member of the flight group from Miami.

Target Palau

There was no relaxing at Majuro. Two days later, on 22 March, this mighty force of flattops, with accompanying warships and support vessels, Task Force 58, with Admiral Spruance in charge, sailed from the Majuro lagoon on what was to be our initiation into battle. Our Task Group 58.1 was under the command of Admiral J. J. Clark. The target was the Palau Island group, south and east of the Philippines.

The Palau Islands had only been viewed by submarines up to this point in the war. They were not yet within the reach of the Allied forces. The objective was to sail southwest toward New Guinea, south of the Carolines, to avoid the arc of possible Japanese search planes, and then surprise the enemy with a swing northward to the Palaus.

It was anticipated there would be a number of Japanese Navy fighting and supply ships in the anchorage there. It was also the objective to neutralize the airfields on Peleliu and Babelthuap so they could not be used as a staging base during an upcoming invasion at Hollandia on the north coast of New Guinea.

It was an impressive fleet that rendezvoused after sailing from the Majuro lagoon. It was embarking on a mission which would find us penetrating enemy waters far beyond any territory challenged thus far in the war. The fleet was composed of two task groups, including five carriers, six battleships, several heavy cruisers, and 22 destroyers which would effectively provide a

116

screen for the two task groups. It was an inspiring array to observe from the air.

Air Group 2 was still in the training phase. So it was, shortly after leaving Majuro, we had one more "group grope" to polish our skills. We did that, with all three squadrons on a simulated attack. We completed our practice dives, proceeded to the rendezvous, and finally made our way back aboard Hornet.

Our secret mission turned out to be not so secret. On 25 March, a Japanese search plane from Truk sighted the fleet, and again the following day during refueling operations. Those sightings produced a change in plans, and it was decided that the attack on Palau would be moved up two days to 30 March.

On March 28, other Japanese search planes had our position well defined. At the same time, we were finalizing plans for our bomb loads and how we could conduct the plan of attack. The Japanese still did not know our objective.

Although hot, the weather was excellent, and the evening sunset was impressive. The sun had just gone below the horizon, but a beautiful rosy glow was still being reflected from the base of the clouds, coloring the sky in a myriad of shades. Turning one's head from west toward the east, the color of the sky changed from red to pink, light green, deep blue, and grey. Small cumulus clouds were merely white spots against a sky of very light blue.

The sea had been as calm as that described by Coleridge in his "Rhyme of the Ancient Mariner." If we had been a sailing vessel, we might well have been as idle as a painted ship on a painted ocean. It was hot on the equator, which we had crossed several times during the day on our zigzag course toward Palau. However, we lowly pollywogs would not become official shellbacks until later, while sailing in safer waters.

Things started to happen on 29 March. It was fairly quiet in the morning, but by late afternoon, bogeys (unidentified aircraft) began to appear on the radar screens. Twin engine Japanese aircraft out there were making aggressive movements toward the fleet. Those planes carried torpedoes. Fighter aircraft were vectored to intercept them, and three Bettys (twin engine Japanese bombers) were shot down.

Figure 47. A good perspective of the Hornet with a part of the air group forward in preparation for recovering the remainder.

We went to general quarters in early afternoon and remained in that condition until nearly midnight. More bogeys made their appearance shortly after dark and proceeded with their torpedo runs. The task group to the north of us was the focus of the attack, but we could see from the flight deck of Hornet the magnificent display of colored flares, flood lights, and anti-aircraft tracer bullets that defined the action.

As a child, I had seen impressive displays of fireworks on the Fourth of July. The events of the evening reminded me of such a display magnified a thousand times. The attacking planes were dropping colored flares and flood lights to outline the ships which were their targets. Five inch anti-aircraft shells were exploding in the sky, and 40 millimeter anti-aircraft batteries were presenting a barrage of shells interspersed with golden orange tracers lacing the sky across the horizon.

We were in an atmosphere of near silence on the flight deck of Hornet as we watched that exciting event. The distance was so great that we could only see the action that was taking place; the sounds of battle could hardly be heard. We mostly heard the sound of a soft breeze coming over the deck and of the bow wave splashing quietly as the ship made its way through those warm south seas. Although the scene was tranquil on Hornet and other ships in our immediate task group, every ship was in a state of readiness to carry out defensive action.

This was our first taste of battle—although indirectly. During the period since we had first come aboard Hornet, we had all thought about the events which we were now observing. The reality of fighting a war was materializing very rapidly.

Although fear was never openly discussed, every individual was confronted with it. We had experienced the death of a fellow cadet and instructor during training at primary base on 22 September 1942. That event had made me aware there would be other deaths, possibly in training (and there were), but inevitably in combat, which we would eventually encounter. Even the deaths of the two crews our squadron lost over West Texas had not really brought forth the realities of the hazards which we would soon experience.

Now was the moment when we had to respond to the question: "How will I react personally to the obligation of performing my duty—to facing the enemy—to carrying out my responsibilities?"

There was the fear of not being brave, the fear of the unknown, the fear of injury or death from any number of possible events. We, as squadron members, did not discuss the subject in those terms. However, I believe we all shared similar concerns and feelings. If there were any doubts, they were not displayed. Fear would not deter one from meeting his obligation to the task at hand and supporting his fellow squadron members.

It would be 45 years later in correspondence with son Steven, that the subject of war would again be examined in detail. It was prompted by an article in The Atlantic Monthly he had read, sending me a copy. With the public's fears focused on nuclear destruction, the article reminded us of what conventional warfare between modern industrial powers is like. It described such a war in a stark and unromantic manner.

My thoughts were summarized in a letter in reply to Steven, written in August, 1989, and refer to The Atlantic Monthly article. This is what I said:

"Perhaps this article revealed to the general public the realities of war as they actually existed. Obviously, the general populous had no idea of what was actually happening. And, even the members of the armed forces, other than the small percentage in the front lines, were unaware of what war was really about. The real war was not glamorous—as many young (and old) people thought. It was tragic for many young people. For those in the Army and Marines who were in active combat, it was a dirty, filthy, devastating, frightening, DANGEROUS experience.

I had no direct contact with a "gory" war. Had seen no missing members—no legs—no arms—no heads— no nothing. It was a clean war for me. A comfortable bunk every night, good food—three meals a day in the ward room. And, in the event a meal was missed because of a mission, there was Roland, our Negro messmate ready to provide a sandwich from the pantry across the passageway from the ready room.

In combat, naval aviators and crewmen either survived or they didn't survive. In our squadron, we only had two or three individuals who received Purple heart awards as survivors. In retrospect, I would still choose the danger of flying aircraft in combat instead of being in the infantry. One did not suffer long if something happened while one was in an airplane. The article discussed in some detail the aspect of fear. Fear was a subject with which every individual was confronted. My diaries revealed some concern about that subject as a cadet in primary training. An instructor and a cadet were killed in the crash of a "Yellow Peril" while we were at our primary training base in Pasco, Washington, in September, 1942. My comment at that time (in my diary) was to the effect that before the war was over there would undoubtedly be many more us meeting the same fate.

That was the first time I truly recognized that death was a very definite possibility. There were other accidents as we progressed through our training, but they were remote and did not have a personal impact. Even a mid-air collision between two planes in our newly formed squadron, with a loss of four people, did not really bring forth the realities of the hazards with which we were being confronted.

As the time came for us to actually enter into physical combat, one of the greatest concerns I had was: "How will I respond personally to performing my duty—to facing the enemy—to carrying out my responsibilities?" There was a fear of my not being brave—a fear of the unknown—a fear of injury or death from any number of possible events. It was not discussed, but I am sure we all shared similar feelings.

I have told you of the conversation I had with Tex Hardin the night before he died. There were other casualties, and they came soon. Along with them, came the subtle fear each time you took off on a mission. However, there wasn't the dramatic fear described in Paul Fussell's article in The Atlantic Monthly about uncontrolled urination or fouling of one's undergarments.

As I made ready for the takeoff and the ensuing mission, there was a persistent feeling in the pit of my stomach—as though I would not want a bite of food again—as though any food in my stomach would not digest. There was an unconscious tightening of every muscle in the body. I could force myself to relax—momentarily. Then, before I knew it, there was that persistent tenseness all over again.

Many of those symptoms were not recognized because of the activities of the moment. There were pre-flight briefings, navigation courses to be plotted, targets to be designated, get up to the flight deck, get the engine started, take off, rendezvous, formation flying—maintaining position. There were a million things. It was only after coming to a moment of complete, forced relaxation, that I realized how tense I had been.

The relaxed condition didn't last long. Next, came the close formation flying as we approached the target—check-off list for the dive—watch for enemy fighters—scout the target area—dive—fear—it was always there.

A sense of elation and a bit of relaxation always followed after completing the attack and getting the squadron together for the flight back to the carrier. There was elation, unless there were some losses. It was back to the carrier—each squadron coming aboard in designated order—each plane coming aboard in the proper sequence.

You came downwind—low—slow—starting a 180 degree turn as you came abreast the fantail—turning all the way—picking up the landing signal officer about 90 degrees from the fantail. This was a tense moment—about 100 feet off the water—five knots above stalling speed—respond to the LSO's signals—in a continuous turn as you came over the fantail—be prepared to land or take a wave-off.

One didn't dare to anticipate a "cut"—instead; one might get a wave-off. With a "cut" your wings were leveled, drop the nose slightly, then bring the tail down—tail hook dragging—engaged—from 80 knots to zero in about three seconds. Get the plane out of the arresting gear and forward of the barriers. Another plane follows a minute behind you.

If you got a wave-off, you had better have flying speed! That was a dangerous situation. Go around and try again. People got killed taking off and landing on the carriers."

On the evening of 29 March, Tex Hardin and I were in the state room he shared with two other pilots. We were discussing the coming events and the hazards associated with our immediate targets and those to come. Tex said, "You know Bill, I don't have the slightest doubt that I will be coming back from the war." My reply was, "Tex, I am absolutely sure that I will too." It was a philosophy which one had to hang on to. Without such a philosophy, we would never have completed the job which we had been trained to do.

Lt.(JG) Carl W. (Tex) Hardin and his gunner would die about 0700 the following morning during an attack on Babelthuap Island in the Palau Group.

General quarters was secured and a traditional steak dinner was served at 2300 that night—the meal before the battle. It was a good meal, but no one was actually hungry. It was to bed, in preparation for a 0430 wake up call. I slept fairly well.

Figure 48. Rear Gunner Jack Secrest (age 19) and the author (age 24) aboard the USS Hornet September 1944.

Combat

Four hours of sleep. To the ready room. Of course, the Skipper's wing would take the first flight. There was the final briefing on targets, navigation tasks were completed, and plotting boards prepared for the flight. Goggles with red lenses were put on a half hour before time to man the aircraft. That would allow the eyes to adjust to the darkness. They would not to be taken off until we were in the cockpits.

We stood around the ready room—sat down—got up, waited. Everyone was demonstrating some anxiety.

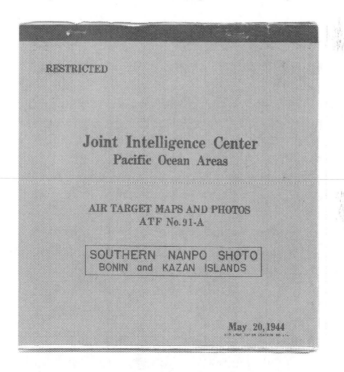

Figure 49. The aerial charts and some pre-strike photos in this book came from a package with this cover sheet that was distributed to air group personnel before each mission.

At 0530 hours the announcement came: "Pilots, man your planes." We made our way out of the ready room, along the catwalk and up the short series of steps to the flight deck. There was a warm humid breeze drifting across the flight deck. Shielded fluorescent lights, recessed in the flight deck, provided some illumination. In the darkness and the subdued lighting, the size of the Beast appeared to be magnified and larger than reality.

Carefully, we maneuvered under and around the parked aircraft before finding our assigned plane, climbing into the cockpit, and preparing for the forthcoming flight. My gunner, Jack Secrest, was more nervous than I. That might have been because of the difference in our ages: he was only 19 years old! After all, I was now twenty three.

It would be more than an hour before daylight. The intention was to conduct a pre-dawn launch, rendezvous, and proceed to the target, attacking shortly after dawn.

We started engines while the ship was sailing down wind. As a result, there was little air flowing over the deck and the large spinners on the propellers further limited airflow through the engine's cylinders. The engines were running near the maximum allowable temperature before we finally came into the wind 45 minutes later. There was no explanation for the delay.

Fighters were launched according to plan. Next came the torpedo planes. One dribbled off the bow and into the water. The right wing of another torpedo plane hit the number two turret while taking off, spun to starboard, and went over the side. All crew members were recovered, but one pilot subsequently died from injuries.

Finally came the bomber's turn. The skipper got off with no apparent problem, followed by Jim McGee. Then it was my turn. *Fly One* went through his wind ups, and I was on my way. The Helldiver rolled slowly down the deck, the fluorescent deck lights passed by at an increasing rate, the tail came up slowly— the end of the deck was near! With the tail pulled down to a three point attitude, we staggered off the bow.

Then, the slow turn to the right to clear the slip stream from the deck, followed by the essential retraction of the landing gear and flaps. With a two thousand pound bomb load, the Helldiver struggled. I got the gear up. Then the flaps were milked up slowly as we gained speed and altitude. The engine temperature, which was at the red line, slowly cooled. Cowl flaps were closed and the airplane was flying.

One member of the flight, Ralph Scheurer, became airborne, but his engine was detonating and was generating less than maximum power. He was about fifty feet above the water and barely maintaining altitude. A reduction in throttle would eliminate the detonation but would also result in a loss of altitude. The problem was solved as the plane slowly settled into the water. The crew was recovered.

Soupy went through the usual routine for a rendezvous, but planes taking off later didn't find us until dawn. It was less than an auspicious beginning. Once the air group had rendezvoused, we headed for our target—the harbor at the south end of Babelthuap.

The flight went well. There were 12 dive bombers, 8 torpedo planes, and 16 fighter escorts. As we came over the target area, our fighters eliminated the token opposition by the enemy fighters. Our only problem was the heavy anti-aircraft fire.

As we approached Babelthuap Harbor at 20,000 feet, cockpit canopies were open; Secrest had rotated his seat so he was facing backward, .30 caliber guns ready to defend against enemy fighters. We could see the lush green foliage, the main harbor, and the lesser bays, but the expected Japanese Navy ships were no longer there. They had escaped two days before. A number of supply ships remained and offered rewarding targets; we took advantage of that opportunity. My target was one of those ships.

We completed our attack, rendezvoused, and returned to our task group. Tex Hardin was no longer with us. None of the flight had seen him after we started our attack. John Houston was shot down on a later flight while attacking targets at the airfield on Peleliu.

Vernon (Mike) Micheel was hit by 40 mm anti-aircraft fire that severely damaged the aircraft and wounded his gunner's left hand, cutting off his left forefinger. The hydraulic system was damaged, no flaps, and the bomb bay doors would not close. Mike managed to land aboard. Dave Stear was also hit. He had a big hole in his wing and no flaps, but he made it aboard. Our first day in combat was a sobering experience.

There were bogeys that evening and night. Fighters shot down a total of 16 enemy planes. None penetrated the screen. General Quarters was secured about 2300 hours, and we were able to hit the sack.

Strikes continued against targets in the Palaus the following day. Fighter opposition diminished, but the anti-aircraft fire was still accurate and intense.

Don Sills was scheduled for an afternoon flight. He had been scheduled for flights on two previous occasions, but each time, as he was in the takeoff spot, the flight was canceled because of problems with the airplane. This time he was determined to go. The airplane was not ready.

Don essentially taxied off the bow. The plane was seen in the water, both Don and his gunner were floating alongside. The guard destroyer came to, launched her motor whale boat and conducted a search without success. Don left a wife and a four month old baby behind. His gunner, Russell McDonald left a pregnant wife. Thirty years later, I would be living in Houston, Texas and meet a good friend of Don's father. The subject was still so painful to Don's father that he would not meet to discuss the event.

Operations in the Palaus were completed; on 2 April we were on our way back to Majuro. We were in a non-combat routine. Anti-submarine patrols continued, and fighters were always on combat air patrol. The destroyers were low on fuel and came alongside for refueling while underway.

Figure 50. The USS Guadalupe refuels the USS Hornet 1944

Refueling was performed by suspending long six or eight inch diameter rubber hoses between the two ships and pumping bunker fuel from Hornet to the destroyer. Fast attack carriers of the Essex class and battleships were used for the refueling of destroyers when tankers were not available. During refueling operations, the bright red Baker (Bravo in the 1990's) flag was flying. The smoking lamp was out and there was no smoking throughout the ship.

During this procedure the ships would proceed on a straight course at a speed of about 15 knots with the destroyer maintaining position on Hornet. The Hornet's band would perform during the refueling operation, positioning themselves where the destroyer's crew could enjoy the music. On these occasions, a five gallon can of ice cream was always transferred via breeches buoy for the pleasure of the destroyer's crew. Smaller ships did not have facilities for making ice cream.

Return to Majuro

As we sailed toward Majuro, and were not under combat conditions, we had the opportunity to explore the ship. The combat information center (CIC) was most impressive! It was here that all of the radar screens, short and long range, were collected. The CIC was in a large compartment with subdued lighting, so the radar screens could be observed most effectively. The screens themselves imparted an eerie greenish light in the semi-dark room and the electronic equipment issued a characteristic odor while providing a constant low level hum.

The short range radar screen showed every ship in the task group and its position relative to Hornet, as well as any aircraft which might be in the area. Long range radar showed ships up to 20 or 30 miles away and aircraft up to 70 or 80 miles if they were at high altitudes. Because WW-2 radars operated on a "line of sight" principle, planes which were at low altitudes could not be detected if they were beyond the horizon.

The position of bogeys (undefined enemy aircraft) was plotted on a large vertical clear plastic screen about eight feet square and one-half inch thick. The screen had the appearance of a large bulls eye with circles, calibrated in miles, from the center. The center represented the ship's position.

A plotter stood behind the screen, with earphones, receiving information from the radar control officer. The plotter made appropriate marks on the back of the screen, showing the direction in magnetic degrees the bogey was from the ship, as well as the estimated altitude. His notations, when viewed from the back, were the mirror image of what was seen from the front of the screen.

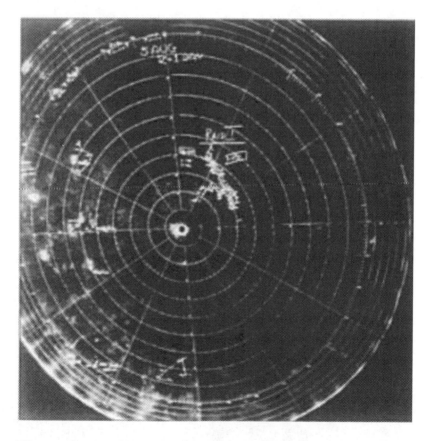

Figure 51. USS Hornet's Radar Plotting Screen August 5, 1944 looks more like a cobweb.

If bogeys were detected, the radar control officer would vector the combat air patrol on a course that would position the fighters favorably for an intercept. That normally brought them toward the bogey slightly to one side and above so a classic attack could be made. The fast attack carriers, which had the latest sophisticated radars, shared responsibility for coordinating defensive action.

The next few days were spent relaxing, sunbathing and getting extra sack time. There were a few anti-submarine patrols and a lot of scuttlebutt about where we were going next. Rumors had us supporting landings somewhere on the New Guinea coast.

Diary—*In a memo to all naval personnel, I was included in a group to be promoted from Ensign to Lt. Junior Grade effective 5 April 1944.*

We entered Majuro Lagoon mid-morning 6 April with all ships riding high, ready to take on fuel. As soon as we anchored, there was a tanker alongside transferring bunker fuel and high octane aviation gasoline. We emptied the tanker, taking on the entire load of bunker fuel and 92,000 gallons of gasoline. The Baker flag was flying, the smoking lamp was out, and the refueling personnel in their purple clothing were conducting the operation.

An ammunition barge followed. Hundreds of bombs were rolled into cargo nets, hoisted to the hangar deck level, and brought aboard. Fresh .50 caliber ammunition was received to replace that which the fighters had expended in air combat and strafing.

Fresh food, including fruit, vegetables, and frozen beef, pork and lamb, was transferred from barges. Those items had been brought thousands of miles from the U.S. in refrigerator ships. That night, Harry Scholar, Aviation Machinist Mate was working on one of our SB2Cs and, as fresh supplies were coming aboard, he thought he smelled the delightful odor of fresh melons. Sure enough, there was a crate of honeydew melons, and the crate had been broken. Harry dexterously removed a melon with his toe, and rolled it, soccer-like to a secluded area of the hangar deck where he could eat it. The melon was so good, he returned for a second one. After all, they were probably being reserved for the officers. The next morning, Harry joined his shipmates for morning chow, who were all enjoying the fresh melons that had just been delivered to the ship.

There were innumerable other items which were required by a crew of three thousand. And, there was the welcome receipt of mail—the first we had received since our departure from Pearl Harbor on 15 March.

It was a period of intense activity! Replacement pilots, gunners, and aircraft were also brought aboard. The pilots were individuals who had had only minimal training since being commissioned and designated Naval Aviators. The gunners were new graduates from Aviation Radioman School. They had not had the experiences which we had enjoyed as members of the squadron since it was formed. A similar procedure occurred every time we returned to an anchorage.

Target Hollandia, New Guinea

We spent three days in Majuro. In spite of the intense activity in the harbor and on the ship, there were few responsibilities for the air group. Weather was warm— occasional rain squalls, huge fluffy white cumulus clouds drifting by. At night, a full tropical moon shone on the low lying white coral islands and the tall, graceful palms leaning out over the lagoon. Under different circumstances, some female companionship would have been most inviting.

Diary—*11 April 1944, Sailed from Majuro with our task group composed of four carriers, Hornet and three carriers of the Independence class—Bellieu Wood,*

Cowpens, and Bataan, along with a contingent of cruisers and destroyers. Our assignment is to support Army landings at Hollandia on the north coast of New Guinea. Our task group will conduct diversion raids, attacking airfields on Wakde, Sawar, and Sarmi about 120 miles to the west of Hollandia, New Guinea.

The Japanese had built an airfield at Hollandia. The Army Air Force would be able to put it to good use. The operation would bypass large forces of Japanese to the east, and at the same time, provide U.S. forces an advanced base from which to launch further attacks toward the Philippines. Our task group's efforts would neutralize airfields which the enemy might use in defense of Hollandia.

Figure 52. Wakde Island airfield, North coast of New Guinea. To be neutralized during the invasion of Hollandia by Naval air forces -April 1944.

**Figure 53. Bombing Squadron Two Pilots aboard the
Hornet**

We were apprehensive about the forthcoming operation. Army Air Force reconnaissance flights had indicated there were up to 350 Japanese aircraft located on three airfields in the Hollandia area. We thought that it could be a difficult engagement. Fortunately, heavy bombardment by Air Force B-24s, catching the Japanese by surprise, destroyed most of those aircraft before we arrived on the scene. The Navy fighters would meet little opposition during our foray along the New Guinea coast.

Our task group was only one of three. The other task groups included a total of four attack and four Independence class carriers. Support ships in those task groups consisted of six battleships and numerous cruisers and destroyers. It was a formidable fleet.

There were two more "group grope" training sessions while we were enroute. We needed them. The air group would eventually become a proficient fighting machine but we certainly weren't there yet.

Refueling took place on 19 April. It would be two days before the invasion of Hollandia. There would be Japanese snoopers; some were shot down by our combat air patrol. General quarters! All preliminaries to the day of battle.

Diary—*21 April General quarters last night when bogeys were picked up on radar. Nothing materialized. It was out of the sack at this morning at 0400 hours to make ready for the pre-dawn launch. Of course, the Skipper's wing will take this flight. Had an excellent breakfast of hotcakes and eggs—then to flight quarters.*

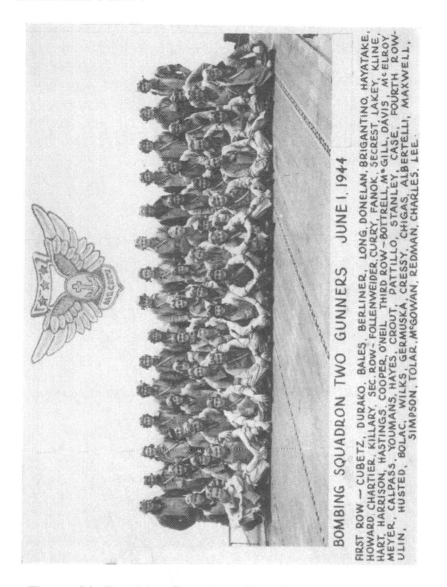

Figure 54. Bombing Squadron Two Gunners June 1944.

Weather was less than desirable. There were squall lines in the vicinity and cumulus clouds went from near the ocean's surface to more than 20,000 feet. The launch and rendezvous went well. We were on our way to attack the airfield on Sawar, an island a few miles offshore from the north coast of New Guinea, 120 miles west of Hollandia. Targets—disable the airport runway and anti-aircraft batteries.

We threaded our way through the squall lines and arrived over Sawar, limited to an altitude of about 10,000 feet because of cloud cover. There was no fighter opposition, and anti-aircraft fire was light. Although, we could see flashes from the anti-aircraft batteries, we saw no indication that their fire was threatening. Our attack was successful and the selected targets appeared to have been destroyed or damaged. After pulling out of our dives, we proceeded about ten miles to the northeast for our rendezvous.

A rapid rendezvous was desired, so defensive fire power could be concentrated in a small area in case enemy fighters appeared. The gunners had been facing the rear with their .30 caliber machine guns at the ready from the time of our approach to the target, through the attack, and the rendezvous.

The rendezvous was accomplished by the lead plane making a sweeping left hand turn at reduced speed at an altitude of about 2000 feet. Succeeding members of the flight could then turn inside of the leader's course and join up on him. When the first section of three planes had been formed, the second section formed below and directly behind. Then, the second division fell in line, flying close formation on the first division. A rendezvous did not require the members of the flight to join up exactly in the sequence they were in before the attack. Those positions could be changed later if so desired.

Soupy arrived over the rendezvous point and started his left hand turn. Jim McGee had joined up on the skipper in the number three position on the right and Henry (Whiskey) Watson joined up in the number two position on the left. I was directly behind and below the skipper, leading the second section. Jack Wells was in the number three position on my right. That left only Walt (Red) Finger to complete the first division.

I looked back to the left and saw Red coming in toward the formation at an excessive speed. When in such a situation, standard procedure called for the incoming plane to slide under the formation to the outside and, after the initial speed had been dissipated, rejoin the formation in the empty slot.

Red didn't do that. He came in very fast on the inside— both his and the gunner's cockpits were open and both occupants could be clearly seen. As they approached, the gunner was giving the "thumbs up" signal. Everything was OK. It wasn't!

At such a high speed, Red tried to slow down by throwing his right wing up. At the same time, he pulled back on the stick. The next events took place instantaneously, but I still remember them as though they were in slow motion.

Red's plane was in perfect alignment below Whiskey Watson. As he pulled back on the stick, the two airplanes came together, the cockpits on the lower plane crumpled like egg shells. The propeller on Red's plane cut into the fuselage of Whiskey's plane just behind the engine mounts. Both planes burst into flames. The engine on the top plane broke off, leaving Whiskey sitting there with nothing in front of him.

As though in slow motion, Whiskey's plane went into a flat spin. After two rotations of the plane, his body left the wreckage. By that time, the plane was inverted and still spinning. Whiskey's body and the plane hit the water at the same time, only a hundred feet apart. A life raft appeared, but there were no survivors.

At the same time, Red's plane fell away from Whiskey's, went into an inverted spin, all the while in a mass of flames. Both planes crashed into the water at the same time. Four men had died in a matter of moments.

The same day, Jesse W. Bamber, USN had engine trouble shortly after takeoff and was making an attempt to get back aboard. The engine quit and Jesse's plane went into the water with wheels and flaps down, tipping the plane over on its back. Jesse was recovered, but his gunner, Leonard Foster, was never found. This would be the first of a number of similar harrowing experiences Jesse would have during the next few months.

Then, Art (Bos) Bosworth crashed on takeoff. He and his gunner were recovered, but Bos had suffered fatal facial and head injuries. Undoubtedly, he had been in the process of retracting the landing gear. In doing so, he had released his shoulder harness, had his head down in the cockpit, lost flying speed, and spun in to the left, hitting the water on his back.

Art Doherty had a prop failure and its speed was limited to 2000 RPM. If he had to take a wave off during landing there wouldn't be enough power to complete the maneuver successfully. As a precaution, he came aboard much too fast. He was still flying when he came to the barriers. His tail hook caught the top cable of one barrier and he knocked down the next three. The plane was a total wreck and was pushed over the side.

Karl Sherwood and gunner were missing after an attack on Sawar. They were not seen after beginning the attack. It had been another difficult day.

Hollandia Support

Operations continued in the Hollandia area. Weather was foul but that did not deter flight operations. Our objective on 23 April was the airfield on the island of Wakde. Cloud cover was such that we had to start our attack from an altitude of only 4000 feet, making us particularly vulnerable to anti-aircraft fire. We dove clean, without dive flaps, released bombs and recovered at about 300-400 feet. It was an uncomfortable situation but we all survived, this time.

There was no fighter opposition in the area, so our fighter escort departed early for the task group. As we were bringing up the rear, we encountered a Japanese Betty—twin engine aircraft—low on the water, on a course 180 degrees from ours. The pilot was trying to be inconspicuous.

Our dive bomber flight, all twelve of us, took up the chase. The Helldiver's speed was only slightly faster than that of the Betty. However, we did slowly catch up, and everyone had the chance to fire some 20 mm shells at the quarry. Finally, three of the flight, Galvin, Garbler, and Schaber, got close enough to set the Betty's starboard engine on fire.

The Betty was trying evasive maneuvers at a very low altitude. In making a left hand turn, the wing tip hit the water, the plane cart wheeled and disintegrated. There was a lot of floating debris, but no sign of life.

The chase had taken us many miles away from the task group and at throttle settings which consumed excessive amounts of fuel. We managed to make it back to the ship and landed aboard, except for Izzie Isabella. He ran out of gasoline and landed near the task group alongside a destroyer. He and his gunner were recovered.

Another Betty, which was snooping, was shot down by the combat air patrol near the task group. A destroyer picked up one survivor who was brought aboard the Hornet via breeches buoy. He had a broken leg, a bullet wound and cut head. However, he received proper medical attention and the prognosis was favorable. He would survive.

I was on anti-sub patrol later in the day. Betty snoopers were picked up on radar and fighters were vectored out on an intercept. I was listening to the radio transmissions between CIC and the fighters during the encounter and could see the action taking place. Two Bettys were shot down, resulting in huge black clouds of smoke. There was a sense of excitement as the enemy planes were shot down and their threat to the task group eliminated.

The next few days were relatively uneventful. There were mopping up operations at Hollandia by the Army and our support operations were no longer required. We did escort tankers and supply ships back to the Admiralty Islands.

General (Dugout Doug) MacArthur's public relations department was extolling the accomplishments of the Army's invasion of Hollandia but there wasn't one word about the Navy's support. MacArthur's nickname was the result of his directing his troops from a hypothetical "dugout" in Australia rather than being out in the field and sharing their dangers and discomfort. Even in those days, he wasn't well liked or admired.

Truk

Instead of our returning to Majuro, Admiral Nimitz had made the decision for the task force to detour through the Carolines and attack Truk, Satawan, and Ponape. Truk was a Japanese stronghold which had been the target of B-24s and a previous carrier strike.

Early on the morning of 29 April, an 84 fighter plane sweep was launched from about 150 miles out for the attack on Truk. This was standard procedure. Enemy fighters would be engaged and eliminated, permitting the dive bombers and torpedo planes to conduct their bombing attacks with a minimum of interference. A total of 59 Japanese fighters were shot down and 34 planes destroyed on the ground during two days of operations.

As usual, the Skipper's division took the first flight. It was another pre-dawn launch with weather which made it difficult for the dive bombers to perform at their best. Heavy cloud cover created a problem in positioning ourselves for an effective dive. On our initial approach, we were under fighter attack, with the Japanese Zeros making their pass, and then pulling up in front of us doing slow rolls. They headed for the large cumulus clouds as our Hellcats went in pursuit.

As we came through a break in the clouds and started our dives on Param Island, there appeared to be nothing but blinking lights in the target area. I knew it wasn't blinking lights—the place was covered with anti-aircraft batteries. I could see many tracers going by, but none were effective.

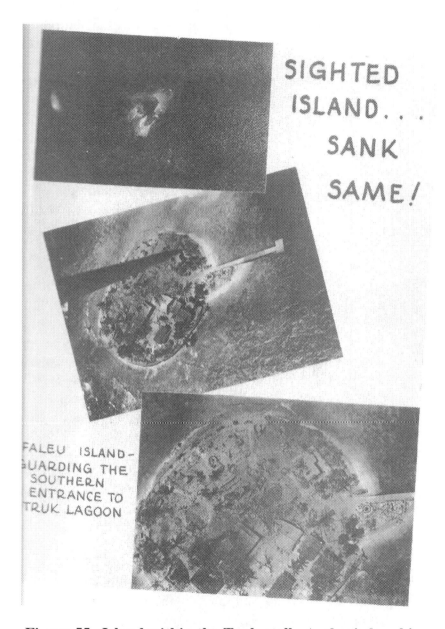

Figure 55. Island within the Truk atoll. Author's bombing attack leaves the island in a state of disarray, 29 April 1944. Strike photo taken by gunner Jack Secrest

In a later flight, three of us were assigned the task of attacking the small island of Falieu. My bomb landed directly in the center of the island, resulting in a truly spectacular explosion which essentially leveled the island. The explosion was undoubtedly caused by an ammunition dump.

It was an exciting two days. Although our squadron had no losses other than some impressive AA damage to aircraft, others in the task force were not as fortunate. A number of our planes were shot down, resulting in several crews being in the water inside the lagoon. Float planes from two battleships landed in the lagoon, recovered many of them, and taxied out to the USS Tang, a submarine assigned to lifeguard duty.

Of 46 airmen shot down from the entire task force, more than half were recovered, 22 of them by Tang. That record would stand for more than a year.

From that point, Truk was useless to the Japanese as a base. Seven supply submarines would be the only vessels to reach Truk during the remainder of the war.

The next several days saw us attacking other bases in the Carolines. There was Dublon—Johnny Fritts came back with his plane all shot up. No flaps, he went into the barriers, over on his back with the airplane on fire. Prompt action by the flight deck crew got the pilot and crewman out of the plane and the fire extinguished. Mike Micheel and Lyle Felderman came back with extensive AA damage but made it aboard.

A sad note this day—"Dad" Taylor came aboard with a 100 pound bomb still in one of the wing racks. It had not released over the target. When Taylor landed, the bomb came loose from the rack, tumbled up the deck and exploded. Two men were killed, several injured, one man had to have both legs amputated

Figure 56. Float planes from the battleships often rescued downed flyers. In this instance following an attack on Truk in April 1944, there were more than could be accommodated by this OS2U Kingfisher. It eventually taxied to a rescue vessel to discharge its "passengers."

At Ponape, there were air strikes with little AA opposition. However, this was an opportunity for some of the cruisers and the six battleships to get in some target practice. They established themselves in "battle line" and fired many rounds of eight and 16 inch shells into targets on Ponape.

After assuring themselves no worthwhile targets remained, they brought the practice to a halt to avoid wasting ammunition. The primary objective of the exercise was to give the ships practice on live targets. It was the first time that the battle line had been able to function as a unit.

After the bombardment of Ponape, the battleships joined our task group. The other two carrier groups had already gone ahead and on that same day arrived at Majuro. Our destination was Kwajalein.

Pollywogs and Shellbacks

Although we had crossed the equator numerous times on both the sorties to the Palaus and to Hollandia, most of us were still officially "Pollywogs." King Neptune had not yet visited the ship and initiated us into the Grand Order of "Shellbacks."

Diary—2 May 1944 This was the day we prepared to receive King Neptune and Davy Jones. Watches were posted throughout the ship to pass the word if they saw King Neptune coming. Uniforms for the occasion were most ridiculous. Burleigh Pattee, all 250 pounds of him—it wasn't muscle—was abreast the island, on the flight deck, in shorts, leather jacket, garters, flying helmet, a parachute, and binoculars. Others were dressed as preposterously. The watch continued throughout the day. Neptune did not arrive.

Diary—3 May 1944 King Neptune came aboard, and all slimy pollywogs were eventually initiated into the Sacred Order of Shellbacks. Since the Pollywogs far outnumbered the Shellbacks, they soon took control. The skipper (Soupy Campbell) was greased down and thrown into a large canvas tank full of water. Jesse W. Bamber, USN received similar treatment, followed by an overnight confinement in a blower room, handcuffed to a pipe. Bob Ricks, "Dad" Taylor, and Johnny Fritts were the culprits of that escapade.

Finally, word came down from the ship's captain that the Pollywog's near mutiny was to cease and desist. It was only then that the Shellbacks were able to continue with the initiation. Some Pollywogs lost their hair, heads were shaved, and everyone had to run the gauntlet, being slapped on the rear end with wet towels. Some were greased down and thrown into the tank. There was a lot of frivolity, but things were carried to an excess in some cases.

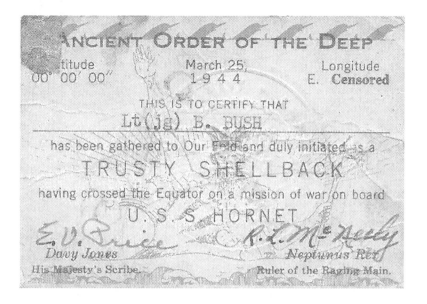

Figure 57. The ancient order of the deep—Billy Bush's official acknowledgement that he is a "shellback" as a member of the USS Hornet on a Mission of war.

King Neptune did not visit all of the ships in the task group on the same day. Although we were sailing in "safe waters," every ship was battle ready. Our initiation into the Grand Order of Shellbacks did not interfere with the primary objective of the group.

The task group sailed into Kwajalein Lagoon at 0800 hours, 4 May. The next month would be a period of relaxation for the air groups. There would be some further training, incorporating the new crews and airplanes that replaced those we lost on the last operation. It would also be a logistical challenge for those supplying the necessities for a massive fleet and the forces which would be going ashore during the upcoming, as yet unannounced, invasion of the Marianas.

If one watched the television series Victory at Sea, this would be the period of soft, soothing music, calm waters, and palm trees bending slightly in a gentle breeze. We had the opportunity to go ashore a couple of times. The Seabees, who were heavily involved with constructing a large airfield, welcomed us. They had a large contingent of men and an Officers' Club which sold cold beer. Two beers was quite a celebration.

Figure 58. Finnell, Vernon (Mike) Micheal, Aldredge, Paul, Garbler, the author (Zinc Oxide nose) Eniwetok, Marshall Is Summer 1944

We saw some of the bunkers and pillboxes the Japanese had constructed as part of the fortifications to defend the island. Many evidences remained of the fighting which had taken place only a few months before. The Japanese were fanatical fighters and refused to surrender: Marines were not interested in taking prisoners. The results were predictable.

On one of the trips ashore, we joined the Seabees again in their "O" club for beer. Afterward we had dinner in their tent-like dining hall. As a friendly overture to a group of aviators who were really fighting the war, they gave us a case of Coca Cola to take back to the ship. Coke was not available aboard ship, and it was a welcome treat.

Back to Majuro

In mid-May, our task group sailed from Kwajalein, and we spent two days honing our skills as an air group. The cruisers did some gunnery practice, firing five inch and 40 mm anti-aircraft shells at towed sleeves. At the end of the exercise we sailed back to Majuro to join the entire Pacific fleet.

We had another two weeks of leisure. I saw my old friend Jack Bohning again. And, by coincidence, at the Majuro Officer's Club I encountered every member, except one, of the flight group with whom I had trained in Miami, a year before. It was late that night before we returned to the ship. The water taxi, a landing craft machine (LCM), capable of handling a truck, or two Jeeps, dropped passengers off at practically every ship along the way to Hornet, which was anchored 11 miles out.

The LCM was like a large box, powered by a rumbling, foul smelling diesel engine. The coxswain was perched aft on a high platform, secured in his station by a sturdy cage of one inch pipe. He could see to the horizon and was in an excellent position to maneuver the craft. It was not propelled smoothly through the water like a speed boat. Every wave encountered on the way created a jolt and resulting spray, which drifted over the bow, sometimes as a mist, and sometimes as a solid sheet of water. It was inevitable. Before the two and one-half hour trip was over, everyone except the coxswain was dripping wet.

The next few days were devoted to loafing. There was a lot of volleyball on the flight deck. And, as part of the entertainment of service personnel, Claude Thornhill and his orchestra performed for the ship's crew. Women entertainers accompanied the show. They received proper attention from the ship's crew.

28 May 1944 came and went without notice. I did not realize my 24th birthday had come and gone.

Samuel E. Morison in his History of the U.S. Naval Operations in World War II, describes in some detail the formation of the Pacific Fleet which was taking place during the period between the Hollandia operation and one which we were anticipating, but knew little about. It was rumored that we would be supporting the invasion of Guam and other islands in the Marianas. The rumors came true.

Target Marianas

The past month had been spent preparing 535 combatant ships and auxiliaries and four and one-half reinforced divisions—127,571 troops, over two thirds of which were Marines, for the invasion of the Marianas. The destination was 1017 miles beyond the nearest advanced base, Eniwetok, and more than 3500 miles from Pearl Harbor.

The vast distances meant that the entire expeditionary force had to be afloat at the same time, and that the ships allotted could do nothing else for at least three months. There was little time to round up the ships, planes, men, and supplies and to decide how every ship and unit was to be employed every day. In an amphibious operation of this magnitude, nothing could be left to chance. Perfect timing was the essence of success.

In early June, it was confirmed that the Marianas were the next objective. Our task group (TF 58.1) would hit Guam on 12 June and spend two days neutralizing Japanese military installations. 15 June had been established as the date for the invasion of Saipan, about 100 miles to the north.

Figure 59. Agana Town, Guam, July 15, 1944 pre-strike photo prior to the invasion by US forces.

After two days at Guam, our task group would move north to Chichi Jima, only 500 miles from Tokyo. Our target would be a seaplane base. The objective—prevent the staging of aircraft south from the main islands. The other three task groups would attack Saipan and Tinian in preparation for the invasion of Saipan.

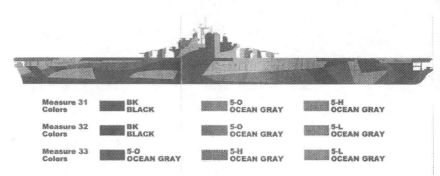

Measure 31 Colors	■■ BK BLACK	■■ 5-O OCEAN GRAY	■■ 5-H OCEAN GRAY
Measure 32 Colors	■■ BK BLACK	■■ 5-O OCEAN GRAY	■■ 5-L OCEAN GRAY
Measure 33 Colors	■■ 5-O OCEAN GRAY	■■ 5-H OCEAN GRAY	■■ 5-L OCEAN GRAY

Figure 60. USS Hornet CV 12 Camouflage Pattern.

On June 6, 1944, in Europe, this was D-Day! The eyes of the world were concentrated on the beaches of Normandy.

On 6 June 1944, a day before, because of the International Date Line, in the western Pacific, we departed Majuro Lagoon, and prepared for the invasion of the Marianas. As author, Samuel Elliot Morison described our sailing:

"A sortie from a coral lagoon is as handsome a naval spectacle as one can find anywhere. In a setting of sparkling blue water, the long reef stretching out of sight, splashed with dazzling white foam, islets covered with the tenderest green foliage and fringed by yellow sands, the battleships, cruisers and destroyers in their fantastic battle camouflage form a column that steams proudly through the pass at 15 knots. With much making and executing of long hoists of brightly colored signal flags, they deploy into a circular cruising formation. Transports are in the center; destroyers on the perimeter throw spray masthead high, commencing their anti-submarine patrol that will never cease as long as the force is at sea."

There were now four fast carrier task groups; TF-58.1 was under the command of Admiral J. J. (Jocko) Clark. It was composed of Hornet, Yorktown, Belleau Wood, Bataan, and support ships. Clark's Flag was in Hornet. Task forces 58.2, 58.3, and 58.4 included an additional five carriers of the Essex class and six of the Independence class.

The fast carrier task groups had the carriers in the center, destroyers on the perimeter. Cruisers, surrounding the carriers, lent anti-aircraft support. We were the attack group, in the forefront, preparing for the invasion of Saipan which the 2nd and 4th Marine Divisions would be conducting in nine days. It was to be a brutal man-to-man battle with few Japanese surrendering, and the Marines taking few prisoners.

Figure 61. Referred to as "Murderer's Row" Six carriers at anchor in Ulithi Atoll late 1944—Wasp, Yorktown, Hornet Hancock, Ticonderoga, Lexingtoon—an impressive sight.

The Marines had departed Pearl Harbor on 29 and 31 May, arriving in Eniwetok on 7 and 8 June. With battleships and other Navy fighting ships as protection, they sailed for Saipan on 12 June. When they got off those transports, after more than two weeks under extremely crowded conditions, it would be for landing on the beaches of Saipan.

The strategy of the Japanese forces during this period was not clearly known, and a complete analysis of their strategy, after the fact, is beyond the scope of this journal.

Briefly, some documents had been captured at Hollandia outlining the Japanese plans in the event of certain actions by the U.S. flcct. Thc Imperial Headquarters realized that the great moment for a decisive naval battle was fast approaching. They were hoping for an engagement in the area of the Palaus and the Western Carolines (Yap and Wolei) as two decisive battle areas.

If the U.S. fleet should appear off the Marianas, it would be assaulted there only by land-based air forces. The Americans would then be lured south into waters where the Japanese fleet could best handle it. The Japanese fleet did not have enough fuel to fight at any greater distance from its base. And, airfields to the west and south would allow Japanese land-based aircraft an excellent opportunity for sinking enemy ships.

The major part of the Mobile Fleet, including Japanese Carrier Division 1, had been in training in Lingga Roads south of Singapore, where fuel from Borneo oil fields was available. Movement of tankers carrying crude oil to the home islands had been severely limited because of attacks by U.S. submarines, requiring the fleet to remain near the source of fuel.

Borneo crude oil was of high quality and could be used as bunker fuel without being processed in a refinery. However, the crude oil contained a high percentage of dissolved, low boiling components. This created an extreme hazard because of the explosive nature of the vapors which were released. As a safety measure the Japanese high command issued orders that the crude oil must be processed before being loaded aboard ship.

Refinery capacity was limitcd. In early May, realizing they had little choice, the Japanese rescinded orders requiring all fuel to be processed. The Fleet was allowed to refuel with Tarakan crude. This decision permitted the shuttle tankers to top off every ship at Tawi Tawi (south and west of the Philippines) and the fleet oilers as well.

Thus, the possible radius of fleet operations was stretched, and by early June, the Japanese Navy felt able to give battle near the Marianas should they turn out to be the American objective. The stage was being set for the coming events. We were on our way. The Japanese were coming out to meet us.

The Japanese forces were composed of three carrier divisions. Cardiv 1 included Zuikaku and Shokaku (veterans of Pearl Harbor, the Coral Sea, and the Eastern Solomons) and the new carrier Taiho, the largest carrier afloat except USS Saratoga. The other two divisions included six flattops and the monstrous twin battleships Yamato and Musashi. There were four older battleships and eleven heavy cruisers that had fought well early in the war. In addition, there were thirty destroyers, some light cruisers and eight to ten tankers.

This group, now cognizant of its mission, steamed through the Visayan Sea toward the San Bernardino Strait and threaded that narrow passage between Samar and Luzon in the Philippines. At that time, Admiral Toyoda repeated the same message by Admiral Togo at the Battle of Tsushima. That was in 1905, when Japanese forces annihilated the Russian Baltic Fleet near the island of Tsushima in the Straits of Korea: "The fate of the Empire rests on this one battle. Every man is expected to do his utmost."

During the evening of 15 June, as the Japanese Fleet sailed into the Philippine Sea, it was sighted and reported by the U.S. submarine Flying Fish. Additional groups of the Japanese Navy were enroute from other areas, joining forces to the east of the Philippines.

In the meantime, Task Force 58 had been enroute to the Marianas. On the morning of the 11th, we encountered snoopers which were shot down by the CAP. At 1300 hours, 200 miles east of Guam, a total of 208 fighters from all four task groups were launched on a fighter sweep over Guam, Saipan, and Tinian. The fighters were supported by eight torpedo and dive bombers carrying life rafts. Two bombers from VB-2 were included and faced fighter opposition but evaded the fighters during the encounter.

Enemy losses were 42 planes destroyed. One of the VF-2 fighter pilots was shot down over Apra Harbor on the west coast of Guam. He was seen in his life raft, drifting out to sea. The fighter attack had been stepped up from a dawn flight on the 12th to the 11th, and it paid off.

That evening, at sunset, Task Force 58.1 continued toward Guam while the other three groups sailed for Saipan and Tinian. On the 12th, the northern task groups were engaging marine and land targets on Saipan and Tinian while Task Force 58.1 was engaged in heavy bombing of Orote Field and other targets on Guam. Our morning had started at 0200 hours: breakfast, then flight quarters at 0300 and off the deck at 0500.

Guam is not a very large island and between the air groups from Yorktown and Hornet, we dominated the military targets. The Yorktown air group hit the airfield on Orote peninsula while the Hornet squadrons attacked targets near Agana Town and to the north. The attacks were well coordinated.

I was diving on five inch anti-aircraft batteries and the long yellow flames emerging from the barrels of their guns were readily observable. They would lash out in a threatening manner, and then rapidly disappear. Attacks continued all day against AA emplacements near Agana Town and on the airfield on Orote Peninsula.

Following the attack, a scouting line was established, flying out to sea on the west side of Guam, searching for Ensign Duff, shot down the day before. He was never found.

The afternoon flight found us over the small island of Rota, to the north of Guam, attacking an airfield and other military installations. There were no problems from the enemy, but on returning to the carrier, my plane experienced a total hydraulic system failure. There were even problems in dropping the landing gear. I finally got the gear down and locked by using unusual attitudes and maneuvers. I followed emergency procedures, but it was not possible to manually pump the hydraulic system up to the necessary pressure to actuate the flaps. I would have to come aboard without them.

Under such circumstances, a plane having trouble was required to wait until all other planes had landed. In addition, there was urgency to get all of the planes on deck as soon as possible so the fleet would not have to maintain a steady course into the wind. I would be the last plane to land. The objective was to get aboard on the first approach.

My first approach was too fast and I got a wave-off. The second approach was acceptable, although still a bit fast. After getting the cut, the plane continued to float. However, there was a quick drop of the nose followed by a rapid dropping of the tail -the engaging of the tail hook—and within seconds the plane had been brought to a smooth halt.

That same day, with his engine producing insufficient power, Dan Galvin settled in off the bow and went into the water. He and his gunner were recovered. Johnny Fritts was not as fortunate. On takeoff, at about 150 feet of altitude, while in a nose high left hand turn just off the bow, the plane stalled. The left wing dropped and the "Beast" was on its back as it went into the water. The gunner was saved, but Johnny never got out. He left a widow.

Diary—June 12, 1944 Our fighters knocked down quite a few of the enemy today. Don't know how many.

We were out of the sack at 0215 hours on 13 June for breakfast and flight quarters at 0330. Even though our wing was not taking a flight until early afternoon, it was to be another busy day. The morning was quiet, but about mid-day, Glen LaMoyne and I were selected, with little notice, for a special mission. We were to lead a group of 20 fighters, each with a 500 pound bomb under one wing and a full belly tank, on a 350-400 mile venture to attack a loitering Japanese convoy to the west of Guam.

Our dive bombers were equipped with additional gasoline tanks in the bomb bays to accommodate the long flight. We would both carry extra life rafts, to provide assistance in the event any of the fighters ended up in the water. I would to do the navigating.

We all took off, rendezvoused, and headed for our target. About 20 miles south of Guam, we received a radio report of a fighter pilot down, in Guam's Apra Harbor. It was one of Fighter Squadron Two's pilots, Donald (Red) Brandt. Don had been hit by anti-aircraft fire when he was at 13,000 feet over Guam. He tried to get the plane out to the west of Guam where the submarine USS Stingray was on station in order to rescue downed pilots. However, he had to bail out too soon and ended up in Apra Harbor.

Glen and his gunner "Don" Donelon were directed to assist by dropping him a life raft. This was accomplished in a professional and successful manner. "Red" was about 400 yards offshore, bobbing around in his life vest, with small arms fire from the beach trying to hit him. Although the rescue submarine was stationed off shore, and the harbor was shallow, Stingray, commanded by LCDR Sam Loomis, Jr. entered the harbor and approached the life raft at periscope depth. The objective was for the pilot to grasp the periscope and be towed to safety. However, "Red's" hands could not maintain a grip on the periscope because of the grease. The submarine made two more passes before "Red" was able to take a strap from the raft and loop it around the periscope for the tow to safety.

Our flight was 40 miles to the west by the time Glen had completed his mission and he was instructed to return to Hornet rather than trying to continue the flight with us.

Weather was unsettled, and it was necessary to navigate around several squall lines to avoid instrument flying conditions. However, after about three hours, we succeeded in locating the Japanese convoy, and the fighters went through their attack. Three of six cargo ships were damaged, and several of the destroyer escorts were strafed.

I circled the convoy at what I thought was a safe distance, and observed the attack. One attentive destroyer escort, observing my circling of the convoy, very accurately fired a five inch anti-aircraft shell in my direction. Fortunately, it was slightly short of its objective. As a matter of discretion, I moved farther from the scene of action.

After the attack, the fighters were anxious to return to the ship and not be delayed by a slow flying dive bomber. The flight leader asked for the course back to the task force and they departed, leaving two fighter escorts to accompany me back to the ship.

There was a feeling of satisfaction in having found the Japanese convoy under the circumstances. There was an even greater feeling of satisfaction as we returned. It had been perfect navigation and after a six and one-half hour flight the southern tip of Guam was just where it should be, as well as Task Force 58.1, fifty miles to the east.

The two fighter pilots and I worked our way into a landing pattern along with the attack groups and came aboard. It had been nothing more than a routine operation. However, as a reward, my gunner and I were given permission to sleep through General Quarters the next morning.

Task Force 58.1 was on its way north toward Iwo Jima and Chichi Jima on 14 June 1944. Hornet was refueling while underway. A tanker on our starboard side was transferring fuel to us, a destroyer on our port side was taking fuel from us. A similar operation was being conducted by Yorktown. The refueling continued until all destroyers and carriers in the task group were topped off. We would be prepared for the attacks on Iwo Jima and Chichi Jima which would be taking place during the next two days. It was a busy operation.

We needed seven new planes and replacement crews for those lost since leaving Majuro on 6 June. The jeep carrier USS Copahee was standing by with both. Six other pilots and I were transferred to Copahee with two exhilarating rides in breeches buoys and a short ride on a destroyer.

A transfer of personnel between ships while underway was accomplished by bringing two ships close together and steaming parallel. Then, a small line was fired from one ship to the other. The first small line was then used to drag a larger line across, capable of carrying heavy loads.

After the larger line was secured on both ships, a canvas basket was suspended from a pulley on the primary line, with smaller lines from the basket to both ships being pulled and released as the passenger was transferred. After entering the basket, the passenger sailed magnificently, 30-40 feet above the surging water, from one ship to the other. Of course, the lines sagged noticeably as one reached the midpoint of the transfer and the water seemed to be lapping at one's feet. However, there were no known losses associated with this interesting procedure.

Aboard Copahee, every square inch of space on the hangar deck and the flight deck was occupied by aircraft. There was even a plane on the catapult ready for launch. We would take that airplane and six more. The only way to fly a plane from Copahee was via the catapult, and that is what we did. Replacement crews and their belongings were taken aboard the destroyer for the trip to Hornet.

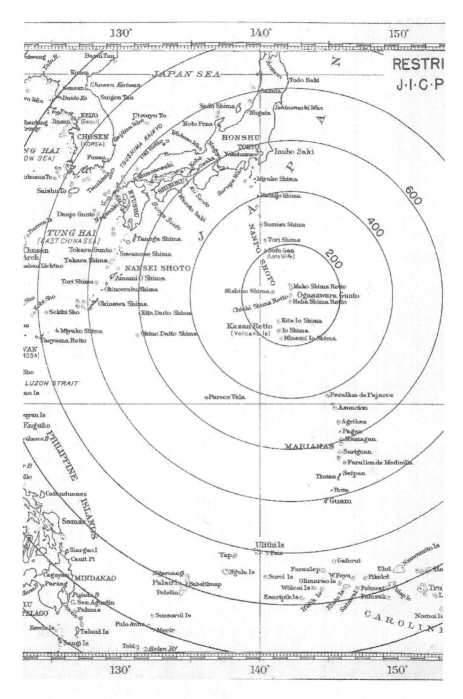

Figure 62. Map shows the position of Iwo Jima and Chichi Jima relative to other locations in the Pacific.

Chichi Jima

15 June 1944—At Chichi Jima we were five hundred miles from downtown Tokyo. It was D-Day for Saipan farther to the south. Weather at Chichi Jima was foul. Numerous squall lines were in the area and clouds ranged from the surface to 20,000 feet. Winds were blowing at Beaufort scale 6-7, heavy seas were running, the ocean surface was solid foam, water was coming over the flight deck, 60 feet above the water line, and even the albatrosses were seeking cover. In future years, fellow pilot John Schaber recalled the great weather we had in the Bonins—the birth place of King Kong.

In spite of the weather, we had a task to perform. Disable the seaplane base at Chichi Jima so the Japanese could not stage any planes from the home islands down to the Marianas during the critical invasions.

Planes were launched carefully to coincide with the rising and falling of the bow. With the bow oscillating about 40 feet from the trough to the crest of the waves, it was necessary for the launching planes to pass over the bow while it was in a level attitude, or just as it continued its rise above the horizon.

The initial attack, including flights from every carrier in the task group, was being led by the air group commander from Yorktown. In retrospect, I think this memorable flight could have been conducted in a much more efficient and logical manner. Our leader took us on a bizarre flight, with altitudes ranging from sea level to 18,000 feet and back to sea level. Squall lines were scouted, explored, flown through, flown around, and eventually conquered. It had taken about two hours to fly to our target, 150 miles away.

Chichi Jima is part of a chain known as the Volcano Islands. It is the remainder of a large volcanic cone which has had one small portion eroded away by the never ceasing pounding of the ocean waves. The interior was a well protected lagoon capable of landing large seaplanes. A maintenance base had been established on one of the few level beaches within the cone, and numerous anti-aircraft batteries had been positioned around the rim.

There was only one direction of attack—approach from the east, confronting intense and accurate anti-aircraft fire as you dove into the cone to attack the assigned target. Escape was through the slot to the west. You were under fire from the very start of the bombing run until you were well out to sea.

On this attack, our target was the machine shop and maintenance areas. Everything went well until I had released my bombs and was heading for the rendezvous area. At that point, some well aimed 20 mm shells went through the right wing just outboard of one of the wing tanks leaving a large gap on the top surface of the wing. The right horizontal stabilizer was also hit. There was a noticeable noise as the shells went through the wing and the stabilizer. It got one's attention.

The airplane continued to fly well, but I had a lingering question whether some fatal damage had occurred that I could not see. If we had gone into the ocean, offshore, there would be no chance of survival. If we landed in the harbor, we would be prisoners of war. After careful observation of the instruments and the engine, the decision was made to attempt a return to the carrier. There was no formal rendezvous, but we all ended up in the same sky flying back to the task group. The weather continued to deteriorate with visibility down to about eight miles. We were on instruments through some of the squall lines.

Obviously, our gasoline supply would be low by the time we got back to the ship. I ran the wing tanks down to a minimum acceptable level and then switched to the reserve tank with 85 gallons left. We had been in the air for five hours by the time we got back, and we were most anxious to get down on the deck.

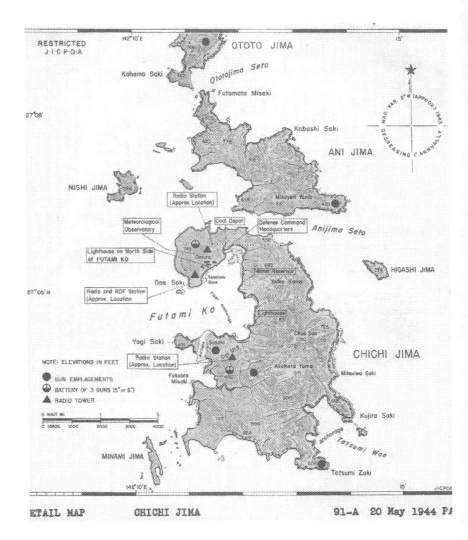

Figure 63. Chichi Jima strike map.

Figure 64. Chichi Jima July 4, 1944 pre-strike aerial photos of military targets.

Figure 65. Top; Chichi Jima from the Southeast .Middle; Chichi Jima military targets Bottom; Torpedo planes approaching.

The task force turned into the wind as soon as we returned. Carriers were ready to land aircraft. From the air, it appeared as though Hornet was motionless in those turbulent waters. Actually the speed of the ship had been reduced to a point where it was barely able to maintain steerage way. Even so, wind over the deck was near 40 knots—a velocity which was barely acceptable for flight operations.

There was no choice. In spite of the adverse conditions—water over the bow, the stern oscillating about 40 feet from the trough to the crest of the waves—we all came aboard in one fashion or another. It was not a classic operation.

Figure 66. In the harbor of Chichi Jima, Hellcats strafe a four-engine Japanese seaplane as highlighted.

As one came around on the final approach, about 100 feet off the water, in a standard rate turn, the fantail was up and then down. Landing procedures called for a steady approach, maintaining a constant altitude in spite of the movement of the ship. You did not dare to "chase the fantail." If the stern was in an unacceptable position when the landing plane arrived at the "cut" point, then it was a wave off and another try.

I was fortunate on my approach. The stern of the ship had reached its maximum height and was rapidly dropping into a trough. I got the "cut" at what would ordinarily be a very high position. However, with the strong wind over the deck there was absolutely no problem in completing the landing. In fact, it was almost like slow motion from the moment of the "cut" until the plane slowly and gently settled on the deck. I had 45 gallons of gasoline in the reserve tank, enough for another 35-40 minutes of flight. Some pilots landed with as little as ten gallons.

Dan Galvin and his gunner, Oscar Long did not return. They were not seen after the beginning of the attack. In spite of the loss of Galvin and his gunner, my diary notation was: "The good Lord was looking out for a lot of Naval Aviators today."

There were more strikes the next day at Iwo Jima where our fighters shot down 17 Zeros. Then, it was time to move south to rendezvous with the other task forces. The Japanese fleet was on its way—we were going to be there to meet them. Tensions were mounting throughout the fleet. This might very well be another Midway!

Figure 67. The rugged coast of Chichi Jima.

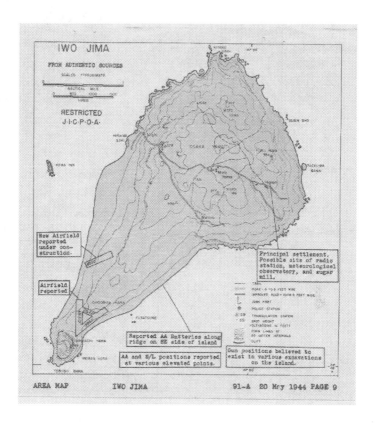

Figure 68. The island of Iwo Jima.

In other parts of the Philippine Sea the Japanese task groups were moving east. U.S. submarines had been able to discern some of those movements. Approximate evaluations of the Japanese fleet size and location had been transmitted to Admiral Spruance, Commander in Chief of Pacific Fleet. Battle strategies on both sides were being carefully reviewed.

On 17 June, the following message was sent from COMSUBPAC to U.S. submarines on station in the Philippine Sea, copied to Task Force 58:

"OUR ESTIMATE OF THE SITUATION IS THAT ALL OF THE MAJOR UNITS OF THE ENEMY FLEET ARE WELL CLEAR OF THE PHILIPPINES AND ARE APPROACHING THE MARIANAS X

CONTACT WITH OUR FLEET MAY BE MADE
TONIGHT OR TOMORROW MORNING X ENEMY
PROBABLY EMPLOYING 9 CARRIERS 6 OR 7
BATTLESHIPS ABOUT 10 CRUISERS AND
NUMEROUS DESTROYERS X IF MAJOR ACTION
TAKES PLACE BADLY DAMAGED ENEMY SHIPS
MAY ATTEMPT TO HEAD NORTH FOR
YOKOSUKA OR BUNGO SUIDO X OTHER
ENEMY SHIPS THAT ARE STILL AFLOAT ARE
EXPECTED TO HEAD FOR DAVAO GULF
TAKING ADVANTAGE OF SHORE BASED AIR
COVER FROM YAP AND PALAU X PIPEFISH
MUSKALLUNGE AND FLYING FISH SEE OTHER
DESPATCHES TONIGHT WHICH ASSIGN YOU
NEW STATIONS TO COVER LINE OF RETREAT
TO DAVAO X

FOR YOUR INFORMATION X THE ABOVE LIST
OF ENEMY SHIPS DOES NOT FRIGHTEN OUR
VARSITY X WE HAVE ALL THAT AND PLENTY
MORE READY AND WAITING AND THEY ARE
ALL ROUGH TOUGH AND NASTY XXX"

That message contributed to the continuous flow of adrenalin as we sailed south. Long range searches to the west continued in an attempt to locate the Japanese fleet. Each flight consisted of two bombers and two escort fighters. There were no radio aids to navigation. At our search mission altitude, we were far beyond the point where we could receive ZB signals. There were no global positioning instruments. The flights were all conducted using "dead reckoning." We carefully observed the compasses, and directional gyros. Our altitudes allowed us to observe the surface and action of the waves, which translated into the velocity and direction of the winds. We flew triangular courses, 350 miles out, 100 miles across and back to the carrier. We did have fundamental radar, operated by our gunners, which was effective only as a "line of sight" instrument. At 2000 feet of altitude, it was effective for about 20 miles. None of our search flights detected the enemy.

When one is 350 miles out and on the cross leg over the ocean, the engine seems to run very rough. As one gets closer to the carrier, the roughness diminishes, and the engine magically runs smoothly particularly when one has the task group in sight.

On 17 June, I was coming inbound on the return leg, about 200 miles away from the carrier on a search mission, when we spotted a large column of black smoke a few miles off our course. On investigating, we saw what appeared to be a small vessel burning to the water line. There was absolutely no sign of life on the vessel or in the water. It was a mystery.

In the meantime, searches were being conducted throughout the Pacific by other task groups and long range patrol planes. Air Force B-24s, Navy PBMs, and Catalinas—all in pursuit of the Japanese fleet. None were successful.

Late on the evening of 17 June, a second contact by submarine Cavalla showed that the Japanese were still coming. At 2115 hours, she sighted "fifteen or more large combatant ships" making 19 or 20 knots on a due east course at lat. 12 deg. 23 min. N. long., 132 deg. 26 min E. This was part of the Japanese Mobile Fleet. The information was received on board Lexington about 0345 hours, 18 June. Darkness prevented Cavalla from seeing the whole fleet and by dawn, for lack of speed, she had lost contact.

The 18th of June was a quiet day. Fighters took the 350 mile searches. Still, we were expecting contact with the Japanese fleet at any moment. Flight crews were standing by, ready to launch an attack as soon as the enemy fleet was located.

In Samuel Morison's "History of United States Naval Operations During World War Two" he stated:

"Not one American search plane sighted a Japanese ship on 18 June. However, about one hour after takeoff, a dawn search mission had encountered three Japanese planes, searching ahead of their fleet. The afternoon search from the American carriers, launched at 1330 hours and covering the sector from NW to S, 325 miles out, found neither plane nor ship. The search planes missed the enemy fleet by about 60 miles. It appeared that the Japanese fleet had not reached a position within 400 miles of Saipan."

The Japanese were more fortunate in their long range searches, having located the U.S. forces which were to the west of Tinian. A flight of 67 planes was scheduled for launch from the carrier Chiyoda at 1640 hours. However, because of confusion in expediting the battle plans, the strike was canceled after only a few planes had been launched. Those planes were recalled.

Japanese strategy on the night of 18-19 June then was to keep the main body of the Mobile fleet about 400 miles and the van about 300 miles from Task Force 58, outside its presumed striking range. The operations plan stressed day attacks with large forces operating beyond the range of U.S. planes. This was excellent strategy, profiting from the greater range of the Japanese aircraft and the presence of their airfields on Guam and Rota, where they might re-arm and refuel. Land planes were supposed to fly in from Yap and Palau to help attack the American carriers.

Admiral Ozawa, commander of the Japanese fleet, had "firmly resolved" to make 19 June the "day of the decisive battle." At 2100 hours 18 June, the Mobile Fleet split course to carry out this plan.

Ozawa's main body, consisting of his own carrier division (Taiho, Shokaku, Zuikaku) and Rear Admiral Joshima's Cardiv 2 (Junyo, Hiyo, Ryubo) changed course to 190 degrees while Admiral Kurita's van, including Cardiv 3 (Chitose, Chiyoda, Zuiho), headed due east. At 0300 hours 19 June they all turned northeasterly and increased speed to 20 knots in order to assume their assigned positions. By 0415 hours 19 June, battle disposition was complete, and everything was set to launch over 300 Japanese planes at the United States task force—still ignorant of the enemy position.

On the American side, all four carrier groups were within sight of each other on the morning of 18 June, and the rendezvous was completed at noon. The three strongest carrier groups, 58.1, 58.2, and 58.3 were twelve miles apart on a north-south line perpendicular to the general wind direction. That allowed any one task group to conduct flight operations without interfering with the others. A battle line, composed of 7 battleships, 4 heavy cruisers, and 14 destroyers was stationed to the leeward, on the enemy side, 15 miles west of flagship Lexington. The weakest carrier task group, TG-58.4, was placed 12 miles north of the battle line to furnish it with air protection.

At noon, the task force turned to a southwesterly course. Flight operations ceased when darkness had fallen and the fleet reversed direction. We had only made good about 115 miles on the WSW course since noon because of the necessity of turning into an easterly wind every time search planes were launched or recovered. Later that evening, intercepted Japanese radio transmissions indicated Ozawa's position to be about 300 miles WSW of the American fleet.

When Spruance received this report, our fleet was increasing the distance from the enemy, and by morning would be in no position to strike him. The optimum launching distance for a plane strike of mixed bombers and fighters was between 150 and 200 miles; the maximum distance considered possible, if the planes were to return, was 300 miles.

Strategy was discussed in great detail that night, and the decision was made to remain close to the Marianas to protect the landings at Saipan and Tinian. There was always the possibility of the enemy making an "end run," catching the landing forces on the beach while our fleet was far to the west. It was better for Task Force 58 to let the enemy strike the first blow. That was not Spruance's choice, but those were the circumstances.

On 19 June 1944, search planes were launched at 0200 hours from Enterprise, flying searches 325 miles to the W by S. By daylight, they would be in an area where they might expect to find the enemy. They unknowingly terminated their search 40 to 50 miles short of the Japanese fleet. Admiralties-based and tender-based searches were unsuccessful. The negative results were exasperating. Enemy snoopers had appeared during the night and escaped. Shortly before 0600 hours, an American plane shot down a snooper only 37 miles SSW of the carrier disposition. Obviously, the enemy was on our heels. Something was bound to happen soon.

Meanwhile, to the west, the submarine USS Albacore, cruising at periscope depth, sighted a large carrier, a cruiser, and the tops of several other ships, seven miles away. Through astute maneuvering, Albacore positioned herself advantageously and at 0910 hours fired a salvo of six torpedoes at the carrier. Albacore had no choice before "going to deep submergence" to avoid three destroyers heading her way.

Albacore did not know that one torpedo struck the starboard side, near the forward gasoline tanks, of Taiho, the newest and largest carrier in the Japanese Navy. This brand new, 33,000 ton, 850 foot ship had just completed launching 42 planes, her share in the second raid of the morning, with the objective of attacking the U.S. Fleet.

The torpedo hit had jammed the forward elevator, and the sump filled with gasoline, water, and fuel oil. However, no fires broke out, and the speed fell off by only one knot from the cruising speed of 27 knots. The flight deck remained clear, and the captain had every expectation that his crew would promptly put this "minor damage" to rights. Ozawa did not take the torpedoing of his flagship very seriously. He was fully confident that damage control and emergency repairs would certainly make her taut and shipshape in short order.

At 1152 hours, submarine USS Cavalla sighted Ozawa's Cardiv 1 about 60 miles beyond Albacore's point of attack. She saw a large carrier with two cruisers and several destroyers. The periscope was raised three times while making an approach, with the destroyer Urakaze abeam all the time. They were not detected. Six torpedoes were fired with a spread that was expected to result in at least four hits. Three hit at 1220 hours.

Shokaku fell out of the formation, with Urakaze standing by. Ruptured gasoline tanks started fires which damage control dealt with promptly, but deadly fumes continued to seep through the ship. At 1500 hours, Cavalla heard explosions and prolonged, monstrous rumblings. They were the death rattles of Shokaku. A bomb had exploded and the big carrier literally fell apart.

Taiho shortly followed her down. The single torpedo hit from Albacore had ruptured one or more of her gasoline tanks. As she steamed to windward at 26 knots, an inexperienced damage-control officer ordered every ventilating duct to be operated at capacity through a wide-open ship, assuming that the draft would blow the fumes away. Instead, the volatile vapors were distributed throughout the vessel. They were not only gasoline vapors, but also volatile components from the Tarakan crude oil, being used as bunker fuel. The necessity of using unrefined crude oil, with its attending hazards, had caught up with Taiho.

At 1532 hours, attempts to pump free gasoline overboard were increasing the danger, and a terrific explosion occurred which heaved up the armored flight deck into something resembling a miniature mountain range, blew out the sides of the hangar, blasted holes in the bottom, and killed everyone in the engine spaces. Taiho went down at 1706 hours with a loss of 1650 men. It would be several months before the U.S. was aware of the loss of this ship.

On 19 June, a flight of land based aircraft was launched from Yap during the early morning to attack U.S. forces west of Guam. They were intercepted and repelled. Four raids were subsequently launched from the Japanese task forces.

Raid One was launched at 0830 hours and had closed to within 72 miles of the U.S. fleet, where they orbited briefly at 20,000 feet in preparation for their attack. Our radar had detected them at 150 miles. At 1023 hours, the U.S. fleet was into the wind, all ships were at General Quarters, flight decks were cleared of bombers, and fighters were launched to engage the enemy. Keep the decks available for fighters to repel attack! At 60 miles from Lexington, our fighters—at 17,000-23,000 feet—TALLYHO!

This was the beginning of the "Great Marianas Turkey Shoot!" Forty-two planes out of 69 Japanese aircraft would fail to return from Raid I.

Raid Two—119 planes launched from Ozawa's carriers at 0856 hours. Warrant Officer Sakio Komatsu, from Taiho, was a casualty after having crashed his plane into the sea, exploding one of the torpedoes from Albacore, surging toward his mother ship. This group was detected by U.S. forces at a distance of 115 miles. Of 128 planes launched, 97 did not return.

Raid Three—Forty-seven planes from Cardiv 2 were launched at 1000-1015 hours. They made fruitless attacks, causing no damage, losing seven. Forty returned to their carriers.

Raid Four— Forty-nine Japanese planes failed to find their targets and headed for Guam. At 1449 hours, when fairly near the island, they jettisoned their bombs. They were picked up on TF- 58 radar screens and Hellcats from Cowpens were vectored out to intercept. The Commander of the U.S. flight reported 40 enemy planes circling Orote Field at Angels 3 (3000 feet) with wheels down.

Cowpens' fighters were joined by more Hellcats from Essex and eight from Hornet. Between them, these 27 F6Fs shot down 30 out of the 49 Japanese planes trying to land. One of Hornet's Hellcats broke into the landing circle of a string of Vals (dive bombers) and knocked down five without damage to himself. The 19 Japanese planes which managed to land on Orote Field were so badly damaged they were beyond repair.

This was a field day for VF-2. They shot down 51 enemy planes. The whole Task Group (58.1) shot down 109. Not one VF-2 fighter pilot was lost. Although, three planes were so severely damaged that they were pushed over the side.

One of the most dramatic events of the day occurred when a VF-2 pilot, Wilbur (Spider) Webb became an ace in a day. While circling a downed pilot in Apra Harbor he glanced back toward Guam. He described the following scene:

"There is a mountain ridge that extends down the center of the island with some peaks 1,000 to 2,000 feet high. Along the ridge tops, barely clearing them was a solid line of aircraft. There were 30 or 40 of them flying in divisions of three, wingtip-to-wingtip. I thought it was strange, because we had no more strikes planned and it was late in the afternoon.

I kept watching and noticed that many of the planes had their landing gear down. The lead divisions were heading straight for me. I was still low over the water:

They banked left, turning on the base leg for Orote Field. When they did, I saw those big red meat balls on the sides of their aircraft. The planes in the lead were Val dive bombers, apparently lower on fuel than the rest, which were Zeros above and behind them.

I never felt so alone in my life—alone in a crowd of our enemy. Then I guess the old flashback from my dad came up: "A time to run and a time to fight." The hard part is to make the right decision at the right time!

I figured the element of surprise and 'doing the impossible' was my only chance to stay alive. By damn, if they got me they were going to have to earn it! I decided to join their traffic pattern. I picked up my mike, called Lieutenant Elliott (the division leader), and told him I was going in alone, and for him to come and help me. I made another transmission and said, "Any American fighter pilot, this is Spider Webb at Orote Peninsula. I have 40 Jap planes surrounded and need a little help."

There followed a breathtaking series of engagements which finalized with Spider receiving credit for downing six of the enemy aircraft, and probably two more. His gun camera ran out of film after the first six. His F6F was so severely damaged that after returning and landing on Hornet, it was pushed overboard. Spider was awarded the Navy Cross for his action that day.

During this day of intense action, the decks were kept clear for fighter action by launching bombers for attacks on Guam. They returned to the carrier only between fighter launches and recoveries. The bomber's task was to keep the enemy airfields inoperative so that Japanese planes could not land or take off. Some of our targets were the anti-aircraft positions which were so prevalent in the area. They did create some problems.

On one attack, Lt.(jg) Lawrence was lost due to anti-aircraft fire. Jesse W. Bamber, USN did it again. During his dive, he was hit in the right wheel well by a large shell which drove through the wing without exploding. It caused a hydraulic fire and created a situation where the plane was temporarily out of control.

Jesse called for his gunner to bail out. His gunner did bail out and was seen descending into the water on the west side of Guam. He was not recovered. Jesse was unable to release himself from entangling cords and oxygen gear but managed to recover from his dive several hundred feet above the ground. The dive flaps on the right side of the airplane were partially split, and the airplane could not make a left hand turn because of the wing damage. Jesse managed to make his way back to the carrier making right hand turns as needed.

Fifty eight years later, Gordon Robertson remembered the occasion. "On 19 June, while in a dive bombing attack on an AA emplacement, I saw that the bomber just ahead of me in the dive had been hit by large caliber AA fire. The plane, smoking, pulled out of his dive, and headed for the harbor nearby. Shortly after clearing the beach, the gunner bailed out. The, the pilot stood up in the cockpit to follow. I flew next to him, and since no fire was visible, I motioned for the pilot to sit down. If he could continue for just a short distance, we would be out of range of shore fire, and his chance of rescue would be greatly improved. The pilot did sit down; the plane did not burn, and was staying airborne. I motioned for him to join up on me to lead him back to Hornet. I landed first, as was our doctrine, in the event the damaged aircraft crashed on deck and fouled it. Although the plane had a large hole in the right wing, the pilot brought it aboard safely. The crewman, who bailed out so close to the beach was never found, although we saw his chute open"

When deck space was available, Jesse was brought aboard in an unorthodox approach. The LSO moved to the starboard side of the after end of the flight deck and brought Jesse aboard from a right hand turn approach. With one wheel down, partial flaps on one side, and with good fortune, Jesse crash landed his plane on the deck of Hornet. There would be more challenges for him in the future.

Thus ended the day. An entry in a Japanese diary captured on Guam described the event from their perspective:

"The enemy, circling overhead, bombed our airfield the whole day long. When evening came, our carrier bombers (Raid IV) returned, but the airfield had been destroyed by the enemy and they ... had to crash ... I was unable to watch dry-eyed. The 'tragedy of war' was never so real."

179

The cost of interdicting Guam was relatively high. Six Hellcats and one bomber (Lt. j.g. Lawrence, with crewman) were missing. Three hundred American carrier planes had been engaged in the interceptions, and an additional number, including the bombers in the fight over Guam. Only 23 had been shot down, and six lost operationally. The net casualties, after rescues: 20 pilots and seven air crewmen killed, together with four officers and 27 enlisted men in three ships hit or experiencing a near-miss.

Seldom have the casualties been so one-sided. The Japanese had thrown 373 planes into their raids and searches. Only 130 returned. In addition, they had lost about 50 Guam-based planes, and others went down in the carriers sunk, or were lost by deck crashes and splashes in the ocean, bringing their total losses on 19 June to about 315. In the two day battle, Japan lost 426 planes and about 445 air crewmen.

By the time darkness fell, the air over Guam—and over the task force too—was clear of enemy planes. The "Great Marianas Turkey Shoot" was over. The U.S. losses on the 19th were 30 planes and 27 pilots/crewmen.

Morison described the event as:

> "The greatest carrier battle of the war. The forces engaged were three to four times those in preceding actions like Midway, and victory was so complete that the Japanese could never again engage on such a scale. From any point of view, the 'Great Marianas Turkey Shoot' of 19 June was a glorious and wonderful battle. The skill, initiative, and intrepid courage of the young aviators made this day one of the high points in the history of the American spirit."

The Philippine Sea

In spite of the euphoria generated by the success of battle, the members of Bombing Squadron Two could not help but reflect on the losses which we had encountered during our tour of duty. The hazards of being a Naval Aviator were becoming more apparent daily. You had to put fear and concern to one side. A big job remained to be done in the near future. However, you realized that if you did it long enough, eventually "they will get you." To this date, we had lost one fourth of our pilots and crewmen to enemy action, and operational accidents.

20 June 1944—The Japanese fleet was out there. Where? Extended search flights were launched. On Hornet and other carriers in TF-58, flight crews were standing by all day in flight gear, ready for launch. In VB-2, "the Skipper's flight will take this one" if and when the enemy is sighted. We were ready!

It wasn't until late afternoon that an Avenger pilot from Enterprise, Lt. R.S. Nelson USNR, became the first carrier pilot in all of those days of searching and fighting to sight a Japanese combatant ship. The contact was made at 1540 hours, at a position estimated to be 225 miles to the northwest. A few minutes later, the position was revised, placing the nearest enemy group over 275 miles from Task Force 58.

The Japanese had intercepted the message Lt. Nelson transmitted to Task Force 58. They knew it was only a matter of time before they would be under attack by U.S. forces.

When we received word of the initial contact—it was about 1600 hours—in the ready room on Hornet, we knew we were about to embark on a mission which was near the maximum range of the Helldiver. The pertinent information was recorded on our plotting boards, and then it was "Pilots, Man Your Planes." This was to be an opportunity that few individuals would ever have.

Flight crews in their flight suits and heavy shoes were out of the ready rooms on the double, chart boards under their arms, pistols in the under-arm holsters and ammunition belts around their waists. They wore the bright yellow life jackets around their necks with attaching straps around the waist and crotch. Oxygen masks dangled from their helmets as they ran across the flight deck to their assigned planes. It was up on the port wing, toes in the step on the side of the aircraft, and into the cockpit.

The plane captains were on the wing, helping the pilots arrange their parachutes and survival back packs. Safety belts, shoulder harnesses, and radio cords were connected and adjusted. An unspoken camaraderie existed between the deck crews and the airmen at moments such as this. There was a common understanding of the forthcoming events.

Preparations on the flight deck allowed no delay. Engines were started. The ship was into the wind and fighter escorts were being launched, followed by the torpedo planes. The dive bombers were last, fourteen of us. As we taxied to the takeoff spot, two officers were holding up large blackboards— the first admonishing, "Get the Carriers first!" and the second with a new position for the Japanese fleet—60 miles further to the northwest. We knew we were in trouble. The "Beast," even under the best of circumstances, would probably not be able to make the roundtrip.

When good friend Jim McGee started to get into his cockpit, he managed to catch both toggles of his life jacket on the canopy track, puncturing the CO_2 bottles and inflating his jacket. He deflated the jacket, but there wasn't time to get replacement CO_2 bottles. Jim took off with a life jacket and empty bottles. That event would nearly cost him his life five hours later.

It was agreed before takeoff that this would not be a standard take off and rendezvous. The skipper would take off and head for the enemy's position at a reduced speed. Other members of the flight would follow, catching up and positioning themselves in the proper formation. A loose formation would be maintained, requiring less manipulation of the throttle and a reduction in fuel consumption.

Jack Secrest, my gunner, and I, took off at 1620 hours with a 1500 pound semi-armor piercing bomb in the bomb bay and two 250 pound general purpose bombs, one under each wing. Those two bombs would create undo drag, increasing fuel consumption. The semi-armor piercing bomb was equipped with a delayed fuse so the bomb could penetrate the armored flight deck of a Japanese carrier and explode in the interior of the ship. Jack was in the back seat, making sure that his twin .30 caliber machine guns were ready for action and that our two man inflatable life raft was ready for any emergency.

It was a normal takeoff. Sluggish. There was the slow, careful turn to the right to clear the deck of prop wash. Then, releasing the shoulder harness, switching hands on the stick—no hand on the throttle—head down in the cockpit, with the right hand grasping for the handle to retract the landing gear—ahh, gear coming up.

Get your head up, secure shoulder harness, left hand on the throttle, start milking up the flaps. Crank the cowl flaps closed. Establish the proper propeller RPM and pitch for climb. Ease back on the throttle mixture from rich to lean—really lean. Watch the cylinder head temperatures to avoid running the engine beyond the red line. Check all instruments to insure the engine is performing properly. Close those canopies. This was going to be a long flight; it would be essential to conserve every drop of fuel.

We were strung out in a long line as we attempted to join up in formation. We got there, but not all of us in our normally assigned positions. I found myself flying in the number three position on Hal Buell, leader of the second division. Dave Stear was in the number two position. Jack Wells was in the second section of Buell's division and Jim McGee was flying wing on the skipper. I didn't know where the others were, but we were all in the formation and headed for one of the most important targets we would ever encounter.

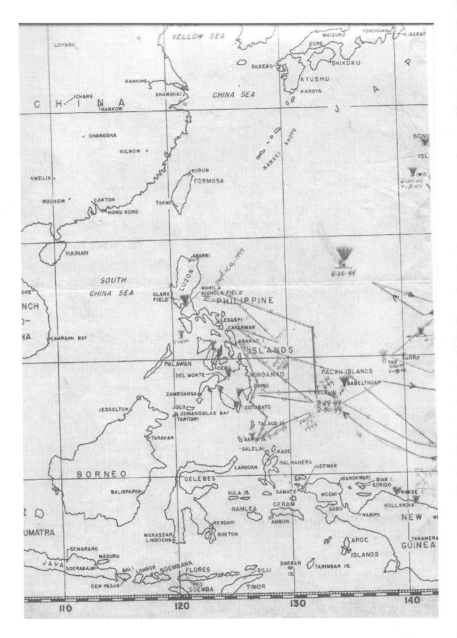

Figure 69. This map shows the various movements of the Task Force during 1944. (Part 1 of 2)

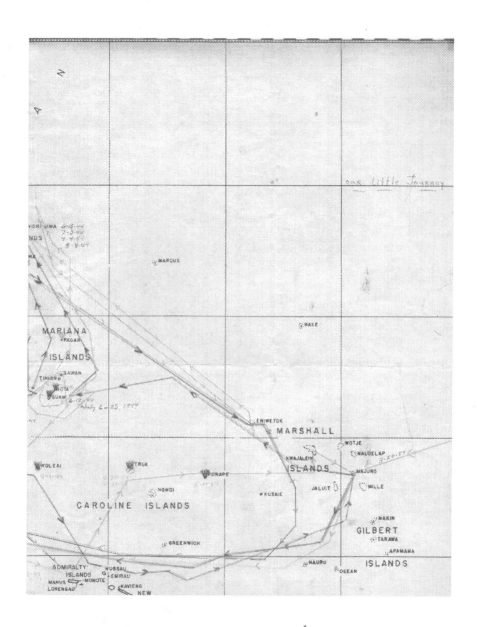

Figure 70. This map shows the various movements of the Task Force during 1944. (Part 2 of 2)

As we slowly headed toward the northwest, our air group formation became more clearly defined. The torpedo planes were slightly below and to one side. The fighters were above, conducting their scissor maneuvers as they moved from side to side, ever ready to resist any enemy attack.

It was hot, we were tense, our oxygen masks were on, perspiration was flowing, and there was very little airflow through the cockpits. Canopies were tightly closed. We flew a loose formation and climbed at a rate which would give us optimum fuel consumption. It would be almost two and one half hours to the reported enemy position and our expected attack altitude of 18,000 feet. It gave us plenty of time to consider the coming events.

As we approached the enemy fleet, it was a scene that only the participants will remember. At our altitude, we could see the setting sun, just barely above the horizon. There was a brand new moon, with a very thin, dim outline; just about to set .The sky was covered with brilliantly colored clouds at altitudes between 3000 and 10000 feet. Surface visibility remained excellent during our approach.

Because our planes were so near the end of their range, we had no time to organize coordinated attacks. Below us was Ozawa's Cardiv 1 with Zuikaku, the only remaining carrier in the group. Thirty six hours earlier his task group had included three of the largest and most threatening carriers in the Japanese fleet. Other Japanese task groups were under attack to the north by U.S. aircraft from other task groups sinking the aircraft carrier Hiyo.

The Japanese ships below us were maneuvering independently and throwing up an intense antiaircraft fire in a spectrum of colors. In addition to the traditional black bursts of antiaircraft fire, with which we were so familiar, there were clouds of blue, yellow, lavender, pink, red and white. Some bursts threw out incendiary particles; some dropped phosphorus streamers. The initial antiaircraft fire was not threatening to our immediate formation; we forged ahead to an advantageous position for attack.

We had climbed to only 16,000 feet rather than the planned 18,000 feet in order to conserve fuel. Our division had achieved a favorable position for attack. Buell called the air group commander on the radio, by-passing our squadron commander, requesting permission to press the attack. Permission was granted.

Figure 71. This picture highlights the number of people on the island who support the launch.

By this time, we were in a close formation, with wingtips only feet apart. Canopies were open, goggles were down, and the diving check off list was complete. Bomb bay doors were open and bombs were armed. The gunners had turned their seats 180 degrees and were seated backward, their machine guns ready for action if necessary to repel enemy planes attacking from the rear.

Buell looked at Dave Stear and then me, and gave a signal with his right hand that was well understood in our squadron. With all fingers pointing downward and the tips coming together in a tight knit position—it indicated a tightening of the sphincter muscle. There were affirmative nods. Yes, the sphincter muscles were tight!

The next few minutes would see a dramatic change in lighting conditions. The sun was setting in the west as we began our attack. There was still sunshine in the cockpits. On the surface, the light was diminishing. Still, the enemy ships and their twisting and turning wakes could be clearly defined, as they maneuvered frantically at flank speed. To the east, twilight was turning to darkness.

Buell passed the lead to Dave Stear, and started his dive. Moments later Dave passed the lead to me and was on his way. Each of us, as we left the formation on our dive, gave a slight waggle of the wings indicating to the next member of the formation that we were on our way. There was only a five second interval between each of us in the first section. Execute the last item on the diving check off list—dive flaps open!

I waited until the last moment before starting my dive to insure the angle of attack would be at the absolute maximum. It would create a more difficult target for the anti-aircraft gunners on the ship which we were attacking. Our standard plan of attack resulted in each member of the flight attacking from a slightly different angle. This would force the enemy to disperse their anti-aircraft fire and reduce the potential hazard to the attacking forces.

As I pushed over, I could see Hal and Dave in their dives. Each of us was rotating counter-clockwise around the target. There were three brilliant cones of antiaircraft tracers originating from the decks of Zuikaku, and each of our planes was diving directly down one of those cones toward its apex—the target. Each bright orange tracer was in sharp contrast to the subdued grey color of the ocean's surface. For every tracer bullet we could see, we knew there were five more bullets that we couldn't see. And, as we dove into the tip of that cone, the anti-aircraft fire became increasingly concentrated. Still, I had the utmost confidence and determination that, "They couldn't hit me."

Figure 72. The Japanese ships below us were maneuvering frantically to avoid our attack and throwing up an intense antiaircraft fire in a spectrum of colors. Zuikaku is in the extreme right center smoking from several bomb hits.

They did hit Hal Buell's plane. He was not downed, but shrapnel did destroy the hydraulic system which prevented the actuation of flaps and landing gear. Shrapnel singed Hal's right shoulder blade, but did not draw blood.

As we left 16,000 feet, sunshine in the cockpit rapidly disappeared. There was a rapid transition of leaving bright daylight and passing into twilight. There was the passage through the cone of bright orange antiaircraft fire—there was Zuikaku in the bomb sight making a right hand turn at flank speed.

My attack brought me over Zuikaku at an angle of 45 degrees from port to starboard about mid-ship. At 2000 feet I released my bombs and was out of the dive at less than 1000 feet. Dive flaps closed! Keep the nose down and head for the surface to present a more difficult target for the antiaircraft gunners.

On looking back, I could see smoke and flames coming from Zuikaku amid-ship. The first three planes down had hit the target. I could not see the impact of my bombs, but following pilots verified direct hits. A certain amount of anxiety remained; we knew that the attack would not be over until we were well clear of the Japanese screen.

Zuikaku had received several bomb hits and five near-misses. The explosions started several fires on the hangar deck which quickly became unmanageable and the order was given to abandon ship. Before it could be completely executed, the damage control party reported progress and the order was rescinded. All fires were subsequently brought under control and Zuikaku managed to limp back to Kure under her own power. Zuikaku never flew another airplane from her deck. However, she was sufficiently repaired to act as a decoy and get sunk in the 25 October battle off Cape Engano in the Philippines.

Immediately following the attack, I was performing evasive maneuvers close to the ocean's surface, making turns and changes in altitude. It was not intentional, but suddenly a cruiser appeared directly in front of me. I bravely armed my 20 mm cannons with the intent of strafing the ship as I passed over it on my way toward our rendezvous point.

When the entire side of the ship erupted in antiaircraft fire, directed toward me, I chose to avoid that challenge. I had a higher priority; escape from the Japanese screen, join up with my companions, head back to Task Force 58 and fight another day. There were some violent maneuvers: up, down, left turn, right turn, and then there was a space between destroyers in the screen. That appeared to be a logical course for me.

After we completed the attack, our fuel supplies were well over half gone. There would be no time for a formal rendezvous. We would join up in twos or threes and make our way back to the fleet. Jack, "Dad" Taylor, and I found ourselves together and turned to the southeast for the next segment of this adventure. This was a birthday gift for "Dad." It was his 23rd birthday.

It was only minutes after I had turned away from the scene of action that the surface twilight turned to darkness. The silvery sliver of moon, which we had seen from 16,000 feet, was over the horizon to the west. The sky was black. The ocean was black. There was no visible horizon. The next two and one-half hours would seem much longer than that. Conversations between my gunner, Jack, and me were limited. We had checked with one another immediately after the attack and were reassured that we were both OK.

In our cockpits, the radium dials of the instruments glowed brightly, activated by ultraviolet light sources on either side of the cockpit. Every needle and every calibration was clearly discernible. The artificial horizon and directional gyro were helpful in determining attitude and direction. Dim blue navigation lights on the upper surface of the wings revealed the relative position of our two planes. The engines droned on. Radio traffic was heavy. The transmissions were invariably negative. "I'm wounded," "I'm low on fuel, going into the water." Numerous other problems were reported.

The Helldiver had four fuel tanks in the wings, two on either side, and a reserve tank in the fuselage. I was going to utilize every available drop of gasoline. Starting with the left outboard tank, I watched the fuel gauge approach empty. When the engine faltered, I switched to the right outboard tank. Next, it was the inboard tanks. When the four wing tanks were empty, it was to the reserve tank.

At 2100 hours, the gasoline gauge for the reserve tank was reading 40 gallons, and the engine was consuming that at a rate of slightly more than one gallon per minute. According to my navigation calculations, Task Force 58 couldn't be more than 50 or 60 miles away. One way or another, this flight was coming to an end.

To the east, we could see what appeared to be lightning bolts. In reality, it was the star shells being fired from the destroyers in our screen, providing direction for the returning planes. Searchlights shortly came into view, brilliant white beams being directed straight up. We came over the battleship Task Force at 500 feet altitude and could barely make out the ship's wakes. As we came upon our Task Group, the carriers had turned on their truck lights, and fluorescent glow lights outlined the flight decks. Red and green running lights were on.

The night was pitch black, and there was no visible horizon. The scene was dramatically colorful, with searchlight beams being directed straight up into the sky, star shells being fired, the red and green running lights on, defining port and starboard, and the many crewman moving hurriedly around the flight decks, attempting to clear crashes. The landing signal officers were on their platforms with reflective orange paddles, performing their ballet, making every effort to get all of the planes aboard. Too frequently there were wave offs because of the fouled decks. Planes had crashed and barriers were down. There was no place to land.

That was the scene I found as I came over Hornet. The deck was fouled. The landing pattern was full of planes searching for a safe haven. There was heavy air traffic over the Task Group. The possibility of a mid-air collision was great. The gasoline gauge for the reserve tank showed 10 gallons remaining. Its accuracy at that level was questionable.

The fighters with their extra 150 gallon belly tanks, and the torpedo bombers with their vast range, could loiter over the carriers and wait for their turn to come aboard. The Helldivers had no choice.

I called Secrest on the inter-com and told him: "Stand by for a water landing." His reply was, "Aye aye, Sir." Caution was the word. There was always the possibility of a midair collision.

We flew to the outer edge of the Task Group to avoid other air traffic and rapidly went through the landing check off list. We were only a few hundred feet above the water. Tail hook and flaps were down, but wheels remained in the retracted position. The parachute harness had been disconnected, shoulder straps locked, the oxygen mask long since removed, and the radio cord disconnected from the helmet.

Fuel supply was on the reserve tank with the needle reading near "empty." Throttle and propeller pitch were set to establish a descent of about 200 feet per minute. Canopies were in the locked open position. The radium dials of the instruments were glowing brightly, showing air speed at about 80 knots. The artificial horizon indicated a slightly nose high attitude and the directional gyro showed a steady course. The surface could not be seen, but when the tail hook started dragging, we knew we were there.

I cut the throttle and pulled the stick full back to get the tail down. It was a very smooth landing. The plane came to a level position and then slowly assumed a nose down position.

Water surrounding the hot engine came to a boil and sizzled for a short while. Then, it was total silence. After a flight of more than five hours, with the sound of the engine and the constant radio traffic, it was a moment of peace and silence which I still remember more than sixty six years later. There was no thought of the 2500 fathoms below. The time was 2130 hours.

There was a very brief moment of relaxation before proceeding to the next task at hand. The plane would not stay afloat very long, in spite of all the empty gasoline tanks.

I climbed out on the port wing and started to inflate my one-man life raft, which was carried in conjunction with the parachute. Secrest was supposed to get out the two-man raft and join me. However, in the moment of excitement, he jumped out on the starboard wing, actuated the CO_2 bottle, inflated the raft, and stepped into it as the plane sank. He didn't get wet.

My life raft inflated slowly, and I was in the water for a few minutes before it was ready for occupancy. We paddled the two rafts together and joined up in the two man raft with all of the survival gear. A destroyer in the screen, the USS Maury, DD 401, had seen us go into the water. It was less than a half-hour before they had come to, and we had paddled over to the ship.

The night was so dark we could not discern whether we were on the port or starboard side of the ship or at the bow or stern. We learned, as we clambered up the cargo nets and came aboard, that we were up forward on the port side.

They treated us royally. There was a lot of talking with members of the crew about events of the day. They provided us with clothing while they washed and dried our flight gear. They scrounged in the galley and provided us with a meal. They found us bunks for the night. As I lay there, I found myself flying that flight several times over. I didn't sleep much that night.

Figure 73. USS Maury DD-401 picked up the author and his gunner the night of 20 June 1944, 200 miles NW of Guam at 2130 hours.

Later, Maury picked up another crew from Bombing Squadron Two. Gus Sonnenberg and his gunner, Dave Killary, had spent eight hours in the water before being rescued. That was fortuitous—almost a miracle.

Dave Killary was keeping a diary at the time, and his notations, after returning to Hornet described their flight.

"At 1600, the Japanese fleet had been contacted. We took off at 1615 hours for the first attack. They were over 300 miles away, and didn't sight them until about 1830. We circled at 16,000 feet and the skipper picked our target—a large carrier. We followed the skipper down through intense ack-ack in a beautiful dive. I blacked out and when I came out of it, one of my ammo cans had the cover ripped off and I had 1,000 rounds of .30 cal. Bullets wrapped around my neck!

I looked back and saw large fires on the carrier, so I'm sure we hit it. They had our altitude and range and the 5" quads were right on our tail, so I called Mr. Sonn on the ICS and he dove down and skimmed along the water until we were out of range. Cruisers and destroyers continued to fire at us, but we were really pouring on the coal and they couldn't reach us."

Gus and Dave subsequently fought off two attacks by Japanese fighters, using an excessive amount of fuel during the encounters. As a result, they were in the water before they could get back to Task Force 58.

Dave continued his description of the following events, their flight that night, low on gasoline, throwing his .30 caliber guns overboard to lighten the load, and finally running out of gasoline. Then, after eight hours in the water, they were picked up by the same destroyer that rescued Jack and me—USS Maury, DD 401.

Ralph Yaussi (pilot) and Jimmy Curry (gunner) both had the same experience—same aircraft—same attack—same return flight—in the water together, but their reports of the attack and its results were entirely different. They both agreed, however, it had been a challenging experience.

There were others who shared in this adventure— individuals from our squadron, others from the Yorktown, in our task group, and in the other task groups. Each one had a story to tell, and memories to last a life time.

A description of the rescue efforts that night are not a part of this journal. Let it be said that the efforts were heroic. Destroyers neglected their anti-submarine duties to rescue pilots and crewmen who were swimming, or were floating in their rubber rafts, with their small blinking waterproof flashlights and the trilling of whistles that aviators carried to attract attention. A search line was established, with destroyers about one-half mile apart, steaming over the course of the returning air crews, to pick up those who had been forced to land in the water.

Because of the extremely difficult night recovery, plane losses on 20 June were much heavier than those of the previous day, but the casualties among aviators were almost the same. The total complement of lost planes was 100 pilots and 109 air crewmen, but 51 and 50 were pulled out of the water that night, leaving 49 and 59 unaccounted for by daylight 21 June. An additional 33 pilots and 26 air crewmen were saved on that and subsequent days. This left the net aviator losses of 16 pilots and 33 crewmen. Hornet was the lucky carrier, losing 21 aircraft but only one pilot and two crewmen, one of whom was killed on Lexington in a deck crash.

Maury was due for refueling the afternoon of 21 June and she came alongside Hornet ready to accept bunker fuel. Secrest and I, along with Sonnenberg and his gunner, Killary, were transferred to Hornet via breeches buoy. I was the first individual of the 14 crews from Bombing Squadron Two, launched the previous day, to return to Hornet. Of those 14 planes, only two were eventually recovered in a flyable condition. On the afternoon of 21 June, the fate of the remaining 12 crews was yet to be determined. Communications in reference to personnel were chaotic. There would be many stories told before the entire picture unfolded.

Hal Buell, leading the attack on Zuikaku, followed by Dave Stear, completed their attack. Hal's plane was damaged by anti-aircraft fire and he experience a singed right shoulder.. The wound proved not to be life threatening. However, the creased shoulder blade created anxieties. Hal and Dave Stear flew back together, finally arriving at Task Force 58.3.

They found Lexington, one of the large Essex class carriers, and managed to work their way into the landing pattern. Dave came around and was given a "cut." He was taxiing forward through the barriers when Hal came up the groove. The barriers were not up.

Hal's hydraulic system was inoperative and he had not been able to get his flaps down. Gravity had brought his landing

197

gear down and into the locked position. He would not be able to retract the landing gear if he was confronted with a water landing. He was fast in the groove and the LSO knew it. Wave off! Although the signal officer had given him the wave off, Hal ignored the signal, and under stress of the moment, took a "cut" on his own. It was in violation of the basic rules of Naval Aviation. His wheels hit the deck, the plane bounced and he was airborne over the barriers at 90 knots.

Dave Stear and his gunner, Redmond, were still in their seats when Buell landed on top of Dave's plane. Redmond was killed instantly. Dave was saved when the propeller stopped turning six inches behind the pilot's cockpit when it struck the armor plating. One of the deck crew was killed and several injured. Hal and his gunner were not injured.

Forty seven years later, Hal wrote a book, "Dauntless Helldiver," describing his exploits as a Naval Aviator. It was done in a manner which revealed the personality that I had remembered from the first time we met. It was as though he had won the war single handed.

He made reference to this particular event indirectly. It was evident that the memory of that event had never gone away. However, in his description of the experience, one who was familiar with the facts recognized his reluctance to accept responsibility for his actions. For one who was not familiar with the facts, there would be a question in reference to what he was writing about. Hal remained with the squadron for the remainder of our tour, fulfilling every responsibility presented to him.

Jim McGee made it back to the fleet and was trying to get aboard one of the large carriers in one of the Task Groups. He came up the groove in a favorable approach but was waved off because of a fouled deck. He had turned left and was parallel with the ship when he ran out of gasoline. If that had happened a few seconds earlier he might well have crashed into the fantail of the ship. Instead, he went into the water wheels down.

The plane was up on its nose, and then on its back. It began to sink almost immediately. Jim was still secured in his safety belt, shoulder harness, and radio cord. He had on the paraphernalia which all air crewmen wore in the event of being downed over enemy territory. He had his gun, ammunition, a hunting knife, heavy shoes, and flight suit. In addition, he had his life jacket with empty CO_2 bottles. It was about 2130 hours and the skies and water were black.

McGee's gunner, Bill Cressy, got out of the plane without difficulty, but Jim was struggling. The plane was probably down 40 feet before he was free and made his way to the surface. He managed to turn on the single cell waterproof flashlight attached to his life jacket, but he was unable to stay afloat, and blow air into the bladders of the life jacket.

A guard destroyer that had seen the plane go into the water, came to, and lowered a motor whale boat in an effort to recover the flight crew. They found Cressy, who told them his pilot was in the water close by. Jim was retrieved with a boat hook from about six feet under when one of the sailors saw the glimmer from his flashlight.

Jim almost died that night. He was returned to Hornet a few days later and spent the next several weeks in sick bay recovering from lung ailments. He subsequently returned to flight duty and completed the tour of duty with the rest of the squadron.

Several days later, all members of the squadron who had taken off for "The Battle of the Philippine Sea" were accounted for except Jack Wells and his gunner. There was little hope that they had survived. No one had seen them after the beginning of the attack on Zuikaku. Jack was married and his wife, Mary, would be having their baby in August.

Jack was a good friend, and I was given the responsibility of inventorying his effects. That procedure consisted of itemizing all of his belongings, packing them in a large wooden cruise box, and preparing them for shipment to his wife. The itemized list was attached to the cruise box.

Among Jack's effects was an eight by ten inch notebook in which he maintained a diary in the form of a personal letter to his wife, written each day. I read only enough to recognize the very personal nature of its contents. The diary included thoughts of love and his expectation of being together again. He also described events of each day, whether it was a daily routine, or the excitement and hazards of going into battle.

Navy rules forbid keeping diaries. They might fall into the hands of the enemy and reveal secret information. Still, some of us did maintain a daily log of our activities. Jack's book went into great detail, and I knew it was something that senior officers might look upon with disapproval. So, being the eternal optimist, and believing I would survive this tour of duty, I decided to maintain possession of the diary. It would be presented to Mary when we returned to the States.

I subsequently did present that precious journal to Mary in October, 1944 after we had returned to the States. I had 30 days leave coming and would spend them in Coeur d'Alene with Margie and friends. On the way, I stopped in Portland, Oregon for a poignant reunion with Mary Wells. I had the pleasure of meeting her two month old daughter and her parents, and spent an overnight with them. It was an opportunity to reminisce. Mary and her parents had an opportunity to learn the intimate details of Jack's last mission.

Every individual who flew that mission had a story to tell. Some were recorded in personal diaries. Others relive the experience in memories. In any event, it was an experience that remains indelibly impressed in one's mind It was an experience that cannot be forgotten.

The War Goes On

The war goes on. More strikes on Guam with the available aircraft. Smitty's wing took a strike on Pagan Island.

Diary— *23 June Garbler got a barrier today and destroyed the airplane. We'll make another tour of Iwo Jima and Chichi Jima before returning to Eniwetok. Bombing Squadron Two is now short 15 planes (out of 36). You can't fight a war that way.*

Diary—*24 June 1944 The fighter squadron went into Iwo Jima on a sweep today, knocking 67 planes out of the sky with only one loss! The entire Task Force shot down more than 100 planes. The Japanese had been in the process of trying to reinforce the Tinian and Guam airfields. Because of foul weather and a delay in repairing airfields on Tinian and Guam, 122 planes had accumulated on Iwo and Chichi Jima. Few of those planes ever flew their intended mission.*

Included in the above engagement were 20 torpedo planes, which made a coordinated attack on the Task Group but were "splashed" by the combat air patrol before they could get within fighting range. Indeed, it had been a productive day.

A shortage of planes would limit bombing attacks on Chichi Jima. Instead of proceeding with the attack, we were ordered to return to Eniwetok. We were in dire need of replacement crews and planes. Scuttlebutt had it that instead of getting all Helldivers as replacements, half the bomber squadron would be getting Hellcats. They would be used as fighter bombers.

That night I suffered my one and only wound of the war. The ship was in a "blacked out" condition and I was wending my way from the ready room, down the ladder and through the hangar deck to my quarters. Normally there were lights on in the hangar deck, but every door which could reveal light to the enemy had to be securely closed before the lights would come on. If the integrity of the "blacked out" condition was disrupted, every light on the hangar deck was automatically turned off. One could get into and out of the hangar deck without interrupting the light system by going through a double door system.

The integrity of the blackout system had been interrupted somewhere that night, and the hangar deck was as black as the inside of the deepest cave. I knew the layout of the hangar deck. I proceeded, through the use of Braille. With hands outstretched, and walking slowly, I could detect the parked aircraft. I was working my way through the hangar deck and toward the living quarter's area, which was lighted.

When I encountered a torpedo bomber, I moved forward of the landing gear, crouched over to avoid the fuselage, and proceeded to the other side. I didn't proceed far enough. As I raised my head, I came in contact with the edge of an open bomb bay door. The upper edge had a rubber gasket which sealed the bomb bay during flight. The lower edge was bare aluminum alloy. The rubber gasket contacted my forehead above the eyebrows and the lower edge contacted the bridge of my nose, leaving a deep cut and voluminous quantities of blood.

When I got back to my room and looked in the mirror, I was impressed. Better report to sick bay and have this thing taken care of. The hospital corpsman didn't seem too impressed. He swabbed the wound, said it was in an area that did not lend itself to stitches, and used a strip of adhesive tape to pull the edges of flesh back together. The scar is still there; embedded in the flesh are the remnants of some black grease not totally removed during the cleansing procedure.

Diary—25 June 1944 Went to church today. It was the first time in over a year. I'll have to go more often.

We entered Eniwetok Lagoon at 1130 hours on 27 June in our usual impressive manner—destroyers offshore as a screen and the larger ships steaming at an impressive 15 knots through the narrow pass. It was a massive array of fighting ships along with support vessels.

The next two days would be busy! Tankers came alongside with bunker fuel and gasoline. Ammunition barges brought bombs and ammunition. Refrigerator ships provided fresh food and vegetables. The U.S. Postal System and its Navy extension delivered mail. Replacement crews reported for duty. Considering there were more than 100,000 individuals to be cared for, it was a marvelous display of logistics at their best!

Figure 74. The SS Guadalupe refueling the USS Hornet while underway. Note the Destroyer USS Maury DD-401 being refueled on the starboard side.

Twenty-one of the bomber pilots went ashore to check out in F6Fs, which would be used as fighter bombers. Alas, it turned out that there weren't enough F6Fs for the fighter squadrons and the bombers too. Bombing-2 would get more SB2Cs, replacing those which were lost during the preceding three weeks. The neophyte fighter/bomber pilots would have to wait.

The word was that we would be getting replacement SB2Cs from a jeep transport carrier, USS Brenton, which was arriving in the area the day of our departure. On 30 June, Task Force 58 was underway. Prior to departure, 14 of us, and 17 fighter pilots were taken via landing craft to the destroyer USS McCall (DD 400), the sister ship of Maury. We sailed, along with the fleet, and rendezvoused with Brenton offshore. After another breeches buoy experience, we were aboard Brenton.

The fighter squadron got 17 brand new F6Fs. We got 14 of the oldest SB2Cs in the Pacific. It was another catapult operation in order to launch planes from Brenton. There were numerous mechanical problems with our replacement aircraft, but they were flyable. The plane I was assigned had a hydraulic system failure, but flaps and landing gear could be actuated using the hand pump. We got them aboard Hornet.

The maintenance crews would have three days to put our new planes in combat readiness before we would again be launching strikes against Iwo and Chichi Jima. By 5 July we would be heading south for pre-invasion strikes against Guam.

This was to be the third trip to the Jimas under the command of Admiral J. J. (Jocko) Clark. Jocko had such an intense interest in subduing the Jimas that some of the aviators caused to be printed certificates of membership in the "Jocko Jima Development Corporation," offering "Choice Locations of all Types in Iwo, Chichi, Haha and Muko Jima, Only 500 miles from Downtown Tokyo." Jocko signed them as "President of the Corporation." I have certificate number 75.

Our two days of inactivity were followed by a fighter sweep over Iwo Jima on 3 July. It was launched from 300 miles out, accompanied by two SB2Cs with extra life rafts. The Task Force fighters claimed 34 downed Japanese planes with a loss of two VF-2 fighter pilots. The Helldivers were attacked by Japanese fighters but they fought them off and returned safely. The next day it would be Chichi Jima's turn.

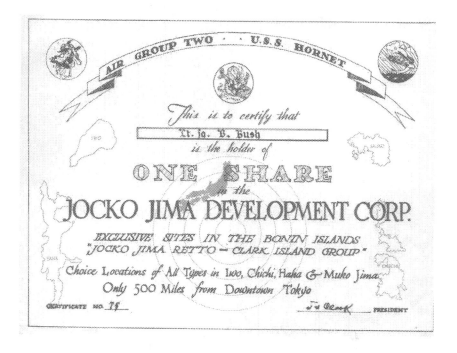

Figure 75. Certificate of Membership # 75 in the "Jocko Jima Development Corporation" (just 500 miles from downtown Tokyo) is owned by Billy Bush.

On the afternoon of 3 July, a new replacement in the bombing squadron, Ensign Bill Connell, was standing in the catwalk outside the bombers' ready room. He had been issued his .38 caliber revolver with its under-arm holster. In the excitement of the moment, with reports of the fighter engagements, he removed the revolver from its holster and brandished it skyward, shouting, "Let me at them!"

The next morning, 4 July 1944, we were up at 0230 hours in preparation for a dawn flight. We were in the same position as we were when we first attacked Chichi Jima in mid-June. The weather was better, but the anti-aircraft fire was just as deadly. I was leading the second section in the Skipper's division and Ensign Connell was on my right in the number three position, flying his first mission. On our approach, a five inch anti-aircraft shell struck Connell's plane in the tail section, separating the tail from the main fuselage. It would have been difficult for the gunner to survive. One parachute was seen leaving the plane. Neither Connell nor the gunner was recovered.

We dove through the slot and attacked our targets. Glen LaMoyne's plane was hit, creating substantial damage in the tail section. In this case, his gunner survived without harm. That was the third time Glen had been hit by AA. He recovered and made it back to the carrier. On coming aboard, two planes couldn't get their tail hooks down. They ended up in the barriers. George Armbruster came aboard fast, bounced and crashed into the barriers. Our wing took a second flight that day for a total of seven hours in the air. On this occasion, everyone returned safely.

For the day—we lost one crew and four airplanes. Tomorrow we head south for pre-invasion attacks on Guam.

5 July was a relaxing day. The flight crews had been given permission to sleep through General Quarters and, other than anti-submarine patrol; there were no flights for the day. Refueling operations for the Task Group took place on 6 July and late in the day a fighter sweep was launched against Guam from 130 miles east of Saipan. The next day, Saipan would officially be declared "secured", after 22 days of fierce fighting.

On the evening of 6 July, the weather was clear and with a full moon, every ship in Task Group 58.1 could be seen as clearly as in the daytime. The North Star was on the horizon. To the south, the Southern Cross was about 30 degrees above the horizon. Occasional huge billowy cumulus clouds could be seen. And, briefly among the clouds, a distinct rainbow, with the definite colors of the spectrum standing out vividly.

Along with the tranquil moments came the reality of the day. We were operating 80 miles to the east of Guam, and when on our missions, even at 1500 feet of altitude, we could clearly see both the Task Group and Guam, when we were half way in between. We flew continuous strikes against the airfields and other military targets. Night fighters attacked targets on Guam and "snoopers" were always targets. Some survivors were picked up and subsequently brought aboard Hornet in handcuffs.

"Sunday, 9 July, church services were held on the bow just below the flight deck. It was a contrast: one group of individuals worshiping God on the forecastle and another group being launched from the flight deck to kill the enemy. I had become a little more faithful in attending church services."

Today, Ensign Al Reynolds, one of our new replacement pilots, came out of his dive, lost aileron control and the plane went into a slow, uncontrolled roll. He managed to get partial control of the airplane and eventually flew it back to the Task Group. There was no way he was going to get it aboard ship or, for that matter, make a controlled landing in the water. He and his gunner bailed out over the Task Group and were picked up by one of the screen destroyers. He was physically and mentally exhausted after the effort of keeping the plane under control on his flight back to the Task Group.

News Item! Radioman First Class Tweed was picked up on the north coast of Guam. He had been a fugitive from the Japanese for two and one-half years after they had captured Guam. He attracted the attention of a U.S. ship by sending signals using a mirror.

Report from Yorktown! One of their Helldivers encountered the same problem that Al Reynolds had. Their pilot and gunner also had to bail out. There are problems with the SB2C aileron control system!

The Task Force moved to the west of Guam and we continued our daily strikes from early morning until late in the evening. It was one week until D-Day, 21 July. The Japanese could only surmise what was happening. There were church services the morning of the 16th. Weather was foul with high winds. We had a movie that evening—Sonja Heine in Everything Happens at Night. (We didn't have movies very often while underway.)

18 July—Continued strikes on Guam. On the last strike of the day, which was expected to be routine, John Powers, on launch careened to starboard. Trouble!! He went through a 20 mm anti-aircraft gun tub, careened over the radio antennas which projected horizontally to the side of the ship, almost flew, but didn't, and spun in to the left. The ship went through the rapid turns to avoid running over the plane and crew and to avoid catching them in the screws. John was recovered but his gunner Thomas F. Charles was not. Thomas was married, left a wife and baby.

Figure 76. Overhead view of the Hornet's mid-flight deck.

Part of my diary notation for the day:

"It is strange. He didn't have any idea anything like that would happen. None of the people it has happened to thought of it. But, one day they are here and the next day they are gone."

In retrospect, I don't believe my analysis was correct. I think everyone thought of the possibility of death, but was unable to visualize himself in the position in which he eventually found himself. The hazards were many, and unpredictable. To this point we had lost one third of our pilots and slightly more than that of our crewmen.

Diary—*19 July 1944 We continued routine strikes on Guam. Our division was assigned antiaircraft targets surrounding Agana town. We were in our dive, the bomb sight was on the target, Secrest was riding backward with his .30 caliber machine guns at the ready in the event of any enemy fighters, 20 mm tracers were all around us. To me, they appeared to be coming up between the wing and the tail section. Jack could see them as they went by him and disappeared in the sky. He picked up the microphone and said, "Mr. Bush, they are shooting at us. We better get the hell out of here!" "Yes Jack, I agree with you." Excitement!! Adrenalin was flowing!*

Air traffic over Guam was heavy. The entire Task Force was conducting attacks on the island in preparation for the invasion, which would occur in two days. Because of the heavy air traffic, it was necessary to get on a schedule to avoid other groups who were attacking their assigned targets.

On this day, Jesse W. Bamber USN did it again. He came aboard fast, never hit the deck, and flew directly into the barrier. The plane was up on its nose, the propeller chewing up the planks in the wooden flight deck. Deck crews were on the scene immediately with CO_2 and other firefighting equipment. There was no fire. No one was hurt. I had watched the entire event from an observation platform high up on the island. It was apparent that Jesse was fast. The LSO erred in giving him a cut, and Jesse made little effort to get that tail hook on the deck. Scratch one airplane.

Mail was delivered today via destroyer while underway. Received 14 letters! How did the mail system function so efficiently?

Diary—D-Day, Guam—21 July 1944—The Skipper's wing took the second strike of the day. We were bombing and strafing the area just inland from the landing beaches. Battleships, cruisers and destroyers were cruising slowly offshore, bombarding the landing areas. Troopships were offshore near the southern landing. Their landing craft were in the water, moving in large circles, creating a continuous frothy wake. The command was given to land troops. Circles of landing craft almost instantaneously became horizontal lines in waves, heading for the landing beaches. The invasion was underway!

The invading forces were new to combat. They had not yet participated in an amphibious landing. The event they were undergoing could never be fully appreciated by others unless they too had shared the same experience. The Japanese, whose days were numbered, were waiting with the intention of killing the invaders. The invaders, with a noble objective, had every intention of killing the Japanese defenders. From the sky, we had only empathy for those in the landing craft.

The initial landings went very well. The Japanese had retreated inland and there was little opposition on the beaches.

As the days progressed, our troops moved inland, resistance strengthened, and it became a dirty war. However, the outcome was never in doubt.

**Figure 77. Jesse W. Bamber, into the barriers—too fast.
July 19, 1944**

The day following the invasion found our carrier and some support ships brazenly anchored three miles offshore to the west of Saipan. We could see the north end of Tinian, and observed the steady U.S. firing of artillery across the straits from Saipan. Destroyers were patrolling the area beyond our anchorage in search of any enemy submarines. We were in need of ammunition and bombs. Those needs were supplied by ammunition barges which came alongside throughout the day.

23 July 1944—We were underway toward Yap, Ulithi and Palau with the intent of interdicting aircraft which might originate in those locations and attack our forces at Saipan, Tinian and Guam. The next week would be spent conducting routine strikes with little air opposition, except for the ever-present antiaircraft threat and the hazards of operational accidents.

27 July 1944—Ensign George Armbruster's plane was seen to roll in an uncontrolled maneuver while in his dive, subsequently crashing into the ground on his back. The "Beast is not trustworthy!" Other air groups had also reported control difficulties with the Helldivers and in this instance; we had been conducting only glide bombing attacks at reduced speeds.

Within days of the loss of Armbruster, a similar event occurred in another air group, but the pilot was able to recover and eventually land the airplane on a friendly airfield. The problem was discovered to be a broken belcrank, a portion of the aileron control system near the wing tip. Emergency action was taken to replace all of the suspect belcranks in Helldivers throughout the fleet. We had no further problems, and our planes were subsequently returned to routine dive bombing operations.

As an air group, we were beginning to lack some of the enthusiasm for fighting the war that we had demonstrated almost five months earlier. It was on 28 July that some of our musician pilots formed an ensemble of guitar, violin, harmonica, and a sweet potato. Other members of the squadron formed a chorus. With the intercom from Ready 2 to the Air Group Commander's quarters turned on, we all struck up the song "Show me the way to go home." His reply was, "I can show you the way but I can't do anything for you."

It would be another two months before we were "shown the way to go home." There would be more challenges. However, either through greater skill in fighting the enemy, managing to avoid fatal operational accidents, or through sheer good luck, we would have far fewer casualties than during our first four months aboard Hornet..

29 July 1944—There was a flight deck parade today to award a purple heart to a fighter pilot who had been hit by a .30 caliber bullet during earlier actions over the Bonins. He had tangled with several Zekes, had been hit in the shoulder, but survived and flew the plane back. Good guy!

**Figure 78. The gear on this Grumman TBF collapsed--
perhaps a hard landing, or battle damage. Flying from
carriers was hazardous to air crew and deck personnel.**

The operations at Guam were going well. Tinian would officially be declared "secured" two days later. Jocko Clark and Task Group 58.1 would be enroute to the Jimas for the fourth visit to the "Jocko Jima Development Corporation." It would be the most profitable.

But first, there was the matter of re-supplying bombs and ammunition. We performed the same brazen act of anchoring off the west coast of Saipan as we had before and bringing ammunition barges alongside. In this instance, the weather did not cooperate. Swells were running high, and attempts to load bombs were creating an extremely hazardous situation. We were able to bring aboard only a part of the anticipated supply. This visit to the Jimas would be conducted with only enough bombs for limited operations.

4 August 1944—Encountered several Japanese ships, and for the Air Group it was almost like shooting ducks. Several Japanese vessels were sunk or damaged. Some of our cruisers and destroyers were detached and ordered to the scene where they sank the remaining ships. This was a much more acceptable target than coming down the slot into the volcanic cone of Chichi Jima where we had been the sitting ducks.

Unfortunately, the torpedo squadron lost the "skipper" of their squadron as he was making a torpedo run on one of the Japanese destroyers. He had previously been hit 14 times by antiaircraft fire. This one was the last. Although the "skipper" was lost, both of his crewmen were rescued.

Searches were being conducted to the north to insure there would be no surprises. The fighters were as close as 140 miles from Tokyo when they encountered a Japanese four-engine seaplane. It was dispatched in a hurry.

Weather thickened and then got worse. Our bomb supply was nearly exhausted. Remaining flights were cancelled, and the Task Group turned to the south for Eniwetok. It was a good feeling. We would be arriving there on 9 August, and we had been assured there would be a three week rest before embarking on our next operation -to make pre-invasion attacks and support landings in the Palaus.

We did arrive in Eniwetok Lagoon on 9 August at 1100 hours. We were to behold the gathering of one of the most impressive displays of naval force in history. There were numerous attack carriers, intermediate size Independence class carriers, Kaiser Coffins, battleships, cruisers, destroyers, troop transports, supply vessels, tankers, submarine and destroyer tenders. Never, in our earlier operations, had we seen such an array! Now, we had a promise of three weeks of rest and relaxation.

We had hardly anchored before a tanker was alongside, ready for refueling. Shortly after, mail call!! Twenty-three letters arrived in two days. Some mail took only one week to arrive from the States and be delivered aboard Hornet. Barges of fresh food were alongside. It had been more than two months since we had had fresh vegetables.

That night we had a meal with flavors and aromas that have lingered for more than 66 years. Can you smell and taste a well baked Russet Burbank potato from the fields of Idaho? With fresh butter? Ahh! How delectable!! This choice was surely superior to the dehydrated food upon which we had survived during the past two months.

New scuttlebutt—Air Group 2 will be relieved after the first phase of the Palau operation (invasion) which is scheduled for the first part of October. We will believe it when it happens.

The next three weeks were spent relaxing. We logged a lot of sack time. There were beach parties with swimming and some beer drinking. One small island was set apart for recreation. We would go ashore, bringing large garbage cans full of ice and canned beer. At the beach, salt water would be added, reducing the temperature of the solution (and of the beer) to near freezing. It was enjoyable.

There was a USO show with five real live girls—and two male singers. They accompanied Claude Thornhill and his orchestra.

Movies—Pin up Girl, not very good really. An Andy Hardy movie—Andy Hardy's Blond Trouble—good looking women. Bing Crosby in "Going my Way"—enjoyed. "Two Girls and a Sailor" with Jimmy Durante, Harry James, Xavier Cugat, Lena Horne and many others. Excellent! Show Business with Eddie Cantor, George Murray, Joan Davis and others. "Bathing Beauties" with Red Skelton and an un-remembered female. "Cover Girl. "

More scuttlebutt—Air Group 2 will go on to the Philippines after the initial Palau operation. Would prefer not.

More beach parties. I took some pictures with the old Kodak camera my grandmother had given to my mother in about 1925. Events of the day were recorded, including some shots of officers from USS Maury DD 401, a ship that will live long in my memory. I went to church several times and wrote many letters.

Diary—21 August 1944 -- Preliminaries are underway, preparing for the next sorties. The Task Group sailed from Enewetok Lagoon to conduct a two day shakedown to maintain air group proficiency.

We still had a number of the "old" Helldivers which had not had the belcranks replaced. We could fly them, but didn't dare place undue strain on them by diving. The immediate objective was to replace them with newer models. Those newer planes were at Majuro. In addition, there were also new Hellcats at Majuro which some of our pilots would be flying as fighter bombers.

After completion of our two day refresher training, the "old" SB2Cs were flown to the beach rather than being brought back aboard ship. On 23 August, a group of us, including Jesse Bamber, USN, went ashore with the intent of flying those planes to Majuro and replacing them with new Helldivers and Hellcats. We got as far as Roi, in the Kwajalein Atoll, where we remained for two days because of foul weather.

While on Roi, I saw my old Marine Corps friend Walt Ottmer. He and I had graduated from Pensacola on the same day and traveled together to Miami for preflight training. We all went to an outdoor movie that night, under the palm trees, and in warm tropical showers.

On 25 August, we flew on to Majuro where we checked out our new airplanes. I was assigned a Hellcat, even though I wouldn't be flying them as a fighter bomber pilot. After

216

studying the flight manual, I had the pleasure of flying a one hour familiarization check flight. The airplane flew well, and I had no problem in taking off, flying or landing.

Figure 79. Beach party with Hal Buell, Looney, Aldredge, Vernon (Mike) Micheel; Eniwetok, Marshall Islands June 1944

The next morning we were on the flight line ready to go—some of us in the new Hellcats and the others in the new Helldivers. Jesse Bamber, USN was in one of the new Hellcats. We were there early for the four and one-half hour flight to Eniwetok.

The flight took off as scheduled. We were all airborne and heading northwest at an altitude of about 10,000 feet where temperatures were moderate. However, about 40 miles northwest of Majuro, Jesse W. Bamber, USN did it again. This would be the last dramatic event with which he would be confronted —except for routine combat flights.

Jesse's engine stopped running. He had no options. He went into the water. There he sat in his small one-man life raft.

Two of us remained behind, circling. We had called Majuro tower and told them of the emergency. They launched a PBY immediately, landed on the calm sea, and had Jesse aboard in short order. My companion and I continued on to Eniwetok without further delay, arriving there shortly after noon. Jesse was subsequently returned via a twin engine land based patrol bomber.

While we were gone, Admiral Marc Mitscher had come aboard Hornet and awarded medals to those who had participated in the "Great Marianas Turkey Shoot" and the "Battle of the Philippine Sea" on 19-20 June. I knew I had been recommended for the Distinguished Flying Cross. Instead, when the awards were issued, nine of us bomber pilots were awarded the Navy Cross, the second highest award issued in the military, just below the Medal of Honor. Although I did not have the pleasure of receiving the award personally, I did receive the paper work and the assurance that a medal would be forthcoming.

More scuttlebutt—Air Group 2 will proceed with operations in the Palaus, go on to the Philippines, and eventually be relieved at Manus Harbor in the Admiralty Islands.

Diary—*28 August 1944 Tomorrow we shove off for Palau and then the Philippines. It is fairly definite that we will be relieved after this operation. We fly a "group grope" tomorrow in our new Helldivers (SB2C-3s). The engines have more horsepower and four-bladed propellers. The fighter bombers will participate in their F6Fs.*

Chow was excellent tonight. Melon, celery stuffed with cream cheese, olives, biscuits, steak, French fries, and carrots. Very good!

Figure 80. The Hornet re-provisioning and R&R at Eniwetok August 26, 1944. Ceremony at which Admiral Mitscher, TF-58 Commander, honored the ship, crew and Air Group 2 for their part in the conquest of the Marianas. USS Essex CV-9 upper left, USS San jacinto (CVL-30) upper right.

We did fly a group grope on 29 August and found the new Helldivers to be better than the originals, but they were still a "Beast." There were other training flights and briefings on targets which we would be attacking in the Palaus and on Mindanao.

Our route was southerly, proceeding south of Truk and along the north coast of New Guinea. We crossed the equator on 1 September.

As usual, there was some apprehension about the forthcoming operation; it was a subject of serious discussion among the squadron members. Talk about being relieved gave one a "shot in the arm." However, caution was the word. News from Europe looks good.

Fighters were launched on a sweep over Palau on 6 September, meeting no opposition. The next day our wing flew two strikes; one on the island of Peleliu, and the other on Angar Island. There was no air opposition, but plenty of anti-aircraft fire. We were in the air 6-7 hours total.

I had achieved sufficient seniority in the squadron, having survived longer than many, so that I was now leading the second division on the Skipper. That was a real challenge. He lacked consideration for his wing men and those who flew in his wing. He flew as though he was the only one in the sky. However, we managed to stay with him.

On our second day at Palau, we didn't launch any Helldivers. The fighter bombers did all of the work. That night the Task Force turned toward the west. On 9 September, we would be conducting strikes against Mindanao.

For a change, the Skipper's wing did not take the first flight. Smitty's wing would take the first flight, Buell's wing the second and we would take the third. By that time we would have an excellent understanding of any problems at hand.

At Mindanao, the skies were ours. We had no air opposition. We spent two days attacking targets on every part of the island. We made milk runs into Davao, on the south side of the island on the Gulf of Davao, where there were primary military targets. I was leading the Skipper's second division and Gus Sonnenberg was leading the second section behind me.

One flight took us 200 miles over 11,000 foot mountains to Cobato on the west side of the island where we attacked inter-island steamers. One hundred and fifty miles of that flight were over rugged jungles and mountainous terrain. Another assignment took us 90 miles over the north coast. Gus Sonnenberg and I found two small ships tied up alongside the dock in a small port. My section took one of the ships, and Gus took the other. When we left, they were both on the bottom. The Japanese would be having a difficult time moving supplies in and out of Mindanao.

The Task Group refueled on 11 September, about 100 miles southwest of Palau. We had originally scheduled six days for attacking Mindanao. However, the first two days had been so successful that the decision was made to move farther to the north. After refueling, we established a position to the east of Samar Island, and started launching strikes 200 miles into Cebu and Los Negros. On our first strike into Cebu, the Skipper's plane developed mechanical problems and he could not take off.

It was my responsibility to lead the flight of nine dive bombers. North of Cebu City, at a distance of more than 200 miles from the ship, we found 30-40 airplanes parked around one of the enemy airfields. We made a dive-bombing attack, the Turkeys came in glide bombing, and the fighters were strafing. Our bombs caused substantial damage, and the fighters had a field day strafing.

As we pulled away, we were attacked by three Japanese fighters making head on-runs. They subsequently broke off their attack when our F6Fs made an appearance. One of our torpedo planes was shot up and a crewman was wounded, but they managed to get the plane back to the ship. The crewman survived. This was a different situation than that over Mindanao.

We continued strikes into Cebu and Los Negros at ranges of 200-250 miles and flight times of about four and one-half hours. Air opposition was taken care of handily by our fighter squadron, which was reassuring. We worked our way south, back to Mindanao and then to Morotai where we lent Douglas McArthur's troops some assistance for their invasion there. Very little resistance was offered by the Japanese at Morotai.

"Rumors—Things have gone so well thus far that we may go on to Manila. On 17 September, we refueled again, southwest of Palau. Then, an ammunition ship came alongside and we transferred bombs to Hornet while underway, using the same technique as for refueling. The tanker had brought Hornet six bags of mail. I received six letters, one of which was from Margie. The Marines are having a tough time at Peleliu. We are heading northwest to Luzon."

On 18 September, the squadrons were briefed on targets we expected to find at Manila. The Japanese had several airfields in the area; airfields that the U.S. Army Air Force had been using before the war. Those airfields were well stocked with enemy fighters and dive bombers. There were more than enough targets to go around. We received our assignments. Our squadron was assigned merchant or naval ships which we expected to find in the harbor. There was little activity that day, but lots of contemplation.

The Task Group rendezvoused with tankers on 19 September, and all ships were "topped off," 270 miles northwest of Palau. Then, we were on our way at flank speed, to be in position 145 miles east of Manila on the morning of the 21st. At flank speed, the ship was throbbing. There was a vibration of the huge shafts driving the screws and one could tell that the engines were generating their maximum power. The cruisers and destroyers were challenged to keep up and maintain position.

Diary—*"20 September 1944 Tomorrow we strike. How many times have I written that phrase? I was nervous. The Japanese have several good airfields in the Manila area and they can launch many fighters. But, with our fighter sweep, and with our escort fighters, we expect to pull it off. The Skipper's wing will take the first strike, naturally. We are on a high speed run for Manila. It will be a 0600 hour launch."*

Figure 81. The author on the wing of an SB2C—September 1944.

On 21 September, we were encountering foul weather! Dense squall lines with large cumulus thunder storms were prevalent in the area. Cells of heavy rain were being encountered and the clouds extended from near the ocean's surface to 30,000 feet. Heavy rains were pelting the carrier's deck, and the crews who were preparing the planes for flight.

The 0600 hour launch was delayed for two hours. When we were launched, we skirted the foul weather, moved across the lush covered mountains of northern Luzon, and then southwest, toward Manila Bay. The harbor was packed with 30 to 40 Japanese Naval and merchant ships. Although we had surprised them, it wasn't long before the sky was filled with antiaircraft fire and enemy fighters.

The AA fire was intense and accurate. They had our altitude defined exactly. Black bursts were covering the sky—all at the same altitude—ours. Some bursts were so close they could be heard, and the residual odor was momentarily present, as we flew through it. Running that gauntlet toward the target was discomforting.

It was a relief when we reached the point from which we could begin our attack. We selected our targets, and went through our dives. Again, it was not possible to observe one's own success in such dive bombing attacks. Looking back, we could see that several ships had been damaged and were possibly sinking. Our next objective was to fly toward Corregidor, rendezvous, and return to our ship on a route that took us just south of Manila.

The Air Group commander from Wasp was the senior aviator aloft that morning. He gave orders for the group to return to the scene of the action and strafe ships as we retreated. I believe he was a relative newcomer to the war. The presence of numerous Japanese fighters (Tonys) making runs on our formation changed his mind. The Tonys were chased off by our F6F's, which shot down nine Tonys and one Zeke. A final report on shipping indicated we had sunk 10 ships and damaged 16.

Our return flight was uneventful. We flew around the thunderstorms, which had diminished somewhat, and returned to a ship with wet decks and a flight deck crew that was soaked from head to toe.

Our attack apparently was a total surprise to the Japanese. Once they knew of our presence, their fighters had become airborne in short order. Manila radio had been broadcasting until about 0930 when it made an announcement of the attack and then left the air.

The next day, the Air Group had four flights scheduled. The Skipper's wing would only take one of those. Foul weather continued, and the schedule was reduced to two flights. Our flight was canceled. I was pleased. Even the Skipper was pleased. Although flight operations were restricted on the second day, the raids on Manila had been tremendously successful.

That same day, a brave Japanese pilot ventured out to the Task Force, penetrated the screen, and made a strafing run on Hornet. He not only made one run, he turned around and came back a second time. The sky was filled with 20 mm and 40 mm AA and he was in the middle of all that. Our anti-aircraft gunners were not successful.

The strafing attack resulted in one American killed and two wounded. There was some easily repaired damage to parked aircraft. Still, such an attack was unsettling.

We refueled again the next day, about 200 miles east of Mindanao. On the 24th, we were at it again in the Central Philippines. Buell's wing was assigned Coron as a target, about 250 miles toward the west side of the Philippines. Wing A, of which I was a member, flew a shorter strike into Los Negros. It was a smooth flight, everything went well.

24 September—Dispatch to Hornet from Cincpac—"Be in Manus harbor, Admiralty Islands, 28 September 1944 for re-

provisioning and to replace Air Group 2." That was a welcome message!

The tour of duty wasn't over yet for Air Group 2. It was 25 September. There were still a few days to go, and there were the routine, humdrum antisubmarine patrols to be conducted. We were about 300 miles northwest of Palau and still exercising every caution to avoid potential submarine attacks.

Our three plane patrol would be catapulted, so the fleet would not have to turn into the wind for a takeoff. I was assigned a plane that resulted in my being the third to launch. Ensign Unsworth, a replacement pilot, was the first on the catapult. His plane was centered over the long steel plate, with the catapult hook ready to run down the 80 foot slot. The bridle, made of large braided cable, was connected over the catapult hook, and to the plane's main landing gear. The catapult system was brought up to pressure, the final check off list was completed, and the engine was at full power. Launch!

There was a serious malfunction in the catapult system, and the plane was thrown off the bow at less than flying speed. Unsworth was in the water before the helmsman could take action to avoid the plane. Sirens sounded as the ship ran over the plane—smoke flares and life rafts went over the side. After a brief period of time Unsworth and his gunner came up, close alongside—only feet from the side of the ship. Miracle! The guard destroyer rapidly came to and recovered the crew. They had both survived an extremely life threatening situation!

I don't remember who was in the second plane to launch, but I believe I knew what his thoughts were. I sat there and watched very intently as the catapult crew lashed the second plane into position. They went through the same procedure as previously. This time the catapult functioned properly and the plane flew.

I had determined that in the event of a second failure they weren't going to get me on that catapult for a third try. That flight was the last for me from the deck of Hornet.

Two days later, there was a flight deck parade, and those of us who had not received awards from Admiral Marc Mitscher were honored in the ceremony. I officially received documentation awarding me the Navy Cross. There would be subsequent awards including a Distinguished Flying Cross and several Air Medals. The ship and the Air Group received the Presidential Unit Citation. In addition, there would be the Asiatic Theater ribbon with four battle stars.

AWARDS AND CITATIONS

PRESENTED BY
Admiral MARC A. MITSCHER

NAVY CROSS

Lt. Cmdr. Campbell	Lt. (jg) Scheurer	Lt. (jg) McGee
Lt. Buell	Lt. (jg) Bush	Lt. (jg) Sonnenberg
Lt. (jg) Taylor	Lt. (jg) Stear	Ens. Looney

DISTINGUISHED FLYING CROSS

Lt. Cmdr. Campbell	Lt. (jg) Ewing	Lt. (jg) Youssi
Ens. Hügel	Lt. (jg) Doherty	Chartier, ARM1/c
Killory, AOM3/c	Kline, ARM2/c	Pattillo, ARM1/c
Secrest, ARM2/c	Hayataka, ARM3/c	Berliner, ARM2/c
Case, ARM2/c	Curry, ARM2/c	Davis, ARM2/c
Lakey, ARM1/c	Cressy, ARM2/c	Begley, ARM2/c

Figure 82. Flight Deck Ceremony, USS Hornet, 26 August 1944. Awarding of medals earned during the "Great Marianas Turkey Shoot" and the "Flight Beyond Darkness" June 19 and 20, 1944. The author received the Navy Cross.

Figure 83. The author (Top row 3rd from right) and other Navy Cross recipients.

When we arrived in Manus Harbor on 28 September, the ship again went through the logistical exercise which had become so familiar. That night the Air Group was honored with a farewell dinner that still stands out in my memory. Within hours of dropping anchor we had a meal of fresh celery, olives, grapefruit, soup, steak, delicious baked Idaho potatoes — mmmm, what a delightful aroma—carrots, ice cream, cake, cheese, raisins, coffee, and for those who wanted them— cigarettes and cigars. Admiral Jocko Clark and Captain Doyle made speeches of appreciation. It was an auspicious farewell!

There would be a few days of waiting at Manus Harbor before the jeep carrier USS Bouganville would arrive, and provide transportation back to Pearl Harbor. We would have no destroyer escort. Fears of Japanese submarine attacks in the waters we would be sailing had diminished to near zero.

At 0900 hours, 7 October 1944, we were underway for Pearl Harbor. Our quarters on the ship consisted of canvas cots located on the hangar deck. We had no assigned responsibilities, and the voyage was a relaxing one, although boring. One balmy, humid evening, I was sitting on the flight deck. A light breeze was drifting over the ship, and I found a spontaneous smile of pleasure had developed on my face. It was similar to that which had occurred in the blackness of the upper berth on the Pullman car in March, 1942. That was when I was returning to Coeur d'Alene, after having passed my physical examination, and being sworn in to the U.S. Navy as an Aviation Cadet. This was many experiences later, and we were going home.

Figure 84. The history of Bombing Squadron Two from commissioning to the end of our tour of duty is a treasured book.

There would be a brief stop in Majuro to pick up some well worn planes. They would be returned to the States for overhaul. I saw Jack Bohning. The next time we were to meet would be in the Administration Building at the University of Idaho in January 1946.

Pearl Harbor provided a week of rest and relaxation. Several of us had the opportunity of staying in a mansion owned by the Fleischmann's of the Fleischmann's Yeast Company. It was located adjacent to the Moana Hotel on Waikiki Beach. Deluxe! Food was excellent and free beverages were provided for all. We visited Honolulu, swam, slept, and really relaxed.

From there it was aboard a troop ship to San Francisco and NAS, Alameda. The squadron was broken up, with some officers being assigned to new squadrons to provide a core of pilots with combat experience. Others remained with Bombing Squadron Two as a nucleus for the new squadron.

Some of us were assigned as Air Department officers on new ships about to be commissioned. Jim McGee and I would be assigned to the USS Cape Gloucester, CVE 109, under construction at the Todd-Pacific Shipyards in Tacoma, Washington.

But first, there was a 30-day leave to be spent back in Coeur d'Alene. Marge and I made the decision to get married. That occurred on 27 January 1945, in the midst of commissioning and shake down operations of the Cape Gloucester. Our experiences during the next four months would be similar to those of thousands of other newlywed couples during the war years.

Marge followed me down the coast to San Diego, as the ship moved in and out of port during the final phase of shakedown. The ship took aboard Marine fighter and torpedo squadrons, and then it was back to the war zones one more time.

This journey took us back to the Philippines and north to Okinawa where the invasion had taken place shortly before. The Marine squadrons were fighting the war, and I was discontented being a member of ship's company.

In early July, I received orders to report to NAS Jacksonville, Florida for night fighter training. On 4 July 1945, I was transferred via breeches buoy from Cape Gloucester to the Navy tanker USS Cache, during refueling operations. Ulithi was the next stop on the way back to the States. Three days after arriving in Ulithi, I was on a civilian tanker, S.S. White Sands, bound for San Pedro, California.

Figure 85. Marge and Billy were married 27 January 1945.

While enroute, White Sands received orders diverting her to Venezuela to pick up a cargo of gasoline. She stopped long enough in Pearl Harbor to drop off her Navy passengers. The troop ship USS Cottle (APA 147) provided transportation from there to San Pedro. Enroute, we heard the first announcement of the dropping of the atomic bomb on Hiroshima.

For those of us returning from the combat zones it was an ecstatic event! The war would be over soon!!

I met Marge in Los Angeles. We had five days' leave and then climbed aboard an air conditioned train bound for Jacksonville, Florida. In San Antonio, Texas, the newspapers proclaimed, in huge headlines, that the war was over! The Japanese had capitulated!!

On arrival in Jacksonville, I was assigned to an outlying field in Green Cove Spring's, where I would be flying F4U Corsairs. It was a sleepy little southern town on the St. John's River, with brick paved streets, and large oak trees filled with long, flowing Spanish moss. We were extremely fortunate to find an upstairs apartment in an old house owned by Charlie and Kathleen Beyers.

The training program wound down. By November, it was completely shut down. We were released from active duty on 11 December 1945, with 33 days of accumulated leave. We were on our way home the next day.

The good Lord takes care of the innocent. In our recently purchased 1938 Plymouth coupe, a Florida car with no heater, worn tires, windows that would not roll up or down, a big hole in the floor board, leaky radiator, no antifreeze, an engine which ran erratically, a mother-in-law as a passenger (who had serious reservations about the young man her daughter had married), and three large bags of oranges; we embarked on a journey diagonally across the United States. We had a map of Florida, with a very small map of the U.S. on the back. This event deserves more attention.

We arrived in Coeur d'Alene, Idaho on 20 December 1945 in time for Christmas. We were ready to start the next adventure in our lives, but that is another interesting story.

Postscripts

It has been more than 68 years since that small group of Aviation Cadets departed from the Pasco, Washington train station on their way to the "Annapolis of the Air." The platform, and the Lewis street underpass, are still there. But, there is no train station. Nor are there any rusty, chipped porcelain reflectors, with bare light bulbs, to greet passengers who might be waiting for a passenger train.

The freight trains and Amtrak passenger trains still roll across the mighty Columbia River on the same four section cantilever bridge, and the tracks still pass to the west of Pasco. The Northern Pacific steam engines have been replaced by huge diesel powered engines and the name on the sides now read, "Burlington Northern Santa Fe."

Water from Lake Roosevelt, behind Grand Coulee dam on the Columbia river, has converted the arid lands of the "Big Bend" country into productive farms which grow thousands of acres of potatoes, corn, onions, melons and grape vineyards. The small communities on both sides of the Columbia River have been transformed into impressive cities. The development of the farm lands has brought a population of migrant workers and Spanish is a second language.

The events and experiences described in "Carrier Pilot" have become ancient history. To succeeding generations, those events have less and less significance. However, the declining number of individuals who were participants in World War Two still remember them clearly, and tend to relive them. It was a moment of pain and glory; an opportunity to serve and to make sacrifices. It was a period when love of country and patriotism were paramount.

Times change. Generations come and go. History fades away, and tomorrow assumes the position of greatest importance.

Figure 86. Alameda California Jan 2002. The author in front of the USS Hornet CV-12

Glossary

At the Dip	Signal flags are hoisted only partially up the lanyard prior to executing a signal. At that point, they are "at the dip."
B-25	A WW-II twin engine bomber, with gull wings built by North American Aviation.
Barriers	Heavy cables, strung across the flight deck, elevated about four feet to prevent into crashing aircraft from proceeding forward parked planes.
Betty	Twin engine Japanese bomber, capable of carrying bombs, or torpedoes.
Bogeys	Unidentified ted aircraft—usually enemy aircraft.
Breeches Buoy	Canvas bag in which personnel, or other items can be transported from one ship to another while underway.
BT-1	Dive bomber, model one, built by Northrop.
Catapult	Hydraulically operated device to propel aircraft into the air in a short distance.
Chandelle	A graceful flight maneuver similar to a "wingover" but with less bank angle.
CIC	Combat Information Center. A compartment on the ship where radar screens are displayed and communications equipment is focused.
CPT	Civilian Pilot Training. A program initiated prior to WWII to training college students.
"Cut"	A signal from the Landing Signal Officer, permitting a pilot to land his plane on the carrier.
CV	A large, attack Navy Aircraft Carrier.
CVE	Escort Carrier built on a merchant hull often used for anti-submarine operations.
CVL	Medium size aircraft carrier built on a cruiser hull.
F6F Hellcat	Navy Fighter, sixth generation, built by Grumman Aircraft.
Fly One	Officer in control of launching aircraft.
Fox Flag	Semaphore flag, indicating status of flight operations. When "at the dip," standby for flight ops. When "two blocked" the ship is conducting flight ops.
Groove	That position above the fantail, from which the landing plane either received a "waveoff" or a "cut".
J-3	Piper Cub Small, High wing 2 place private plane. Used for

	primary training.
Knot	One nautical mile per hour—6076 feet.
LCM	Landing Craft Machine can carry personnel or equipment from ship to shore.
LSO	Landing Signal Officer—directs planes as they make an approach to landing on an aircraft carrier.
N2S	Second generation primary training plane. Ordinarily painted yellow and referred to as the "Yellow Peril." Generation built by Stearman (Boeing).
N3N	Third generation primary training plane. Built at the Naval Aircraft Factory in Philadelphia, Pa. Also painted yellow and referred to as the "Yellow Peril"
"O" club	Officer's club.
OS2U	Observation and search plane. Second generation built buy Consolidated Aircraft Co. Catapult launched from cruisers and battleships.
Port Side	Left side of the ship when facing the bow.
Polliwog	Individual who had sailed across the equator, but had not yet been initiated into the "Sacred Order of Shellbacks."
PBM	Twin engine Patrol Bomber seaplane built by Martin Aircraft Co.
PBY	Twin engine Patrol Bomber built by Consolidated Aircraft Co. Later models were amphibious.
Ready Room	Quarters for flight crews during flight operations and routine activities.
SBC	Scout Bomber built by Curtiss Aircraft Co. First generation to be called "Helldiver".
SB2C	Scout Bomber built by Curtiss. Second generation "Helldiver" also called "The Beast."
Starboard	Right side of the ship when facing the bow.
Shellback	A person who had sailed across the equator and had been initiated into the "Sacred Order of Shellbacks."
SBD	Scout Bomber built by Douglas Aircraft Co. Primary US Navy dive bomber until 1944.
SNJ	Advanced traininer built by North American Aviation Co. Constant speed prop.
SNV	Basic Trainer built by Vultee Aircraft Co. Two speed prop.
TF	Task Force designation such as TF-58.1
Turkey	Affectionate name for the Grumman TBF torpedo bomber.

Tony   Japanese Fighter.

Two Block   To run signal flags from the "dip" position on to the halyard
                to maximum height—signal to execute the maneuver.
Val   Japanese dive bomber.

UPF7   Two place biplane built by the WACO Aircraft Co. used for
                advanced training in the CPT
Wingover   An aerobatic maneuver in which the plane is brought into a
                90 degree back during climbing/descending turn.
Yellow Peril   Primary trainers for new flight students painted yellow to
                make them more observable.